Dialogues on the Ethics of Capital Punishment

**New
Dialogues in
Philosophy**

*A series in dialogue form, explicating foundational problems in the philosophy
of existence, knowledge, and value*

Series Editor
Professor Dale Jacquette, Senior Professorial Chair in Theoretical Philosophy, University of Bern, Switzerland

In the tradition of Plato, Berkeley, Hume, and other great philosophical dramatists, Rowman & Littlefield presents an exciting new series of philosophical dialogues. This innovative series has been conceived to encourage a deeper understanding of philosophy through the literary device of lively argument in scripted dialogues, a pedagogic method that is proven effective in helping students to understand challenging concepts while demonstrating the merits and shortcomings of philosophical positions displaying a wide variety of structure and content. Each volume is compact and affordable, written by a respected scholar whose expertise informs each dialogue, and presents a range of positions through its characters' voices that will resonate with students' interests while encouraging them to engage in philosophical dialogue themselves.

Dialogues on the Ethics of Capital Punishment

Dale Jacquette

ROWMAN & LITTLEFIELD PUBLISHERS, INC.
Lanham • Boulder • New York • Toronto • Plymouth, UK

ROWMAN & LITTLEFIELD PUBLISHERS, INC.

Published in the United States of America
by Rowman & Littlefield Publishers, Inc.
A wholly owned subsidary of The Rowman & Littlefield Publishing Group, Inc.
4501 Forbes Boulevard, Suite 200, Lanham, Maryland 20706
www.rowmanlittlefield.com

Estover Road
Plymouth PL6 7PY
United Kingdom

British Library Cataloguing in Publication Information Available

Library of Congress Cataloging-in-Publication Data:

Jacquette, Dale.
  Dialogues on the ethics of capital punishment / Dale Jacquette.
    p. cm. — (New dialogues in philosophy)
  ISBN-13: 978-0-7425-6143-4 (cloth : alk. paper)
  ISBN-10: 0-7425-6143-7 (cloth : alk. paper)
  eISBN-10: 0-7425-6386-3
  eISBN-13: 978-0-7425-6386-5
  1. Capital punishment—Moral and ethical aspects. I. Title.
  HV8694.J33 2009
  172'.2—dc22   2008028148

Printed in the United States of America

♾™ The paper used in this publication meets the minimum requirements of
American National Standard for Information Sciences—Permanence of Paper
for Printed Library Materials, ANSI/NISO Z39.48-1992.

For the souls of all the innocents
lost on death row
and the victims of all the guilty

If we are to abolish the death penalty, I should like to see the first step taken by my friends the murderers.

—Jean-Baptiste Alphonse Karr (1808–1890)

Capital Punishment is a silly excuse for fear. The police fear the guy so they say "Off with his head!" Not only is it morally wrong, but it's medieval!

—Walt Whitman (1819–1892)

Contents

1

⌒❦⌒

Day One: Matters of Life and Death

A coffee shop in a university town; a corner table. Cars passing by outside in the street, and New Age music, acoustic guitar, piano, and oboe playing at low volume in the background. Two students, a man and a woman, are sipping coffee and tea and poring over a newspaper.

C: Look at this. Another execution last night in Texas, and two more scheduled for the day after tomorrow in Florida.

P: I saw that. Here's one that happened in Japan. A man killed his whole family with a hammer.

C: That's awful, of course. What I can't believe is that the death penalty is still practiced in civilized countries.

P: Why not? Depending on what you mean by a "civilized country." If you look at history, the vast majority of civilizations have imposed capital punishment for certain kinds of crimes. We think of ancient Greece as one of the most civilized places that existed at any time in the world, in some ways the birthplace of our modern democratic civilization. That didn't stop the Greeks from executing Socrates for corrupting the youth of Athens and failing to honor the city's gods. The irony, really the Socratic irony, is that such a decision was precisely the kind of action Socrates expected of a democracy and one of the reasons why he rejected democratic government in favor of an aristocracy of "the one who knows." Didn't you read Plato's *Republic* last semester? Socrates asks if you needed medical attention whether you would follow the advice of an expert qualified to diagnose and cure disease, or take a vote at the marketplace of whoever happens to be standing around, and then do whatever they might think was best. He says if that seems like the wrong way to address the health of the body, how much more important should it be for the one who knows rather than the many to govern the state.

C: Well, that's just my point. What the Athenians did to Socrates was morally wrong. Almost everyone agrees that he was unjustly killed, probably for political reasons, precisely because of his widely known opposition to democracy. I would say it is unethical to execute anyone for any crime, let alone for whatever threat Socrates' ideas might have been imagined to create for the stability of the city-state. That, after all, is what Socrates was accused of. He didn't kill anyone or steal anything from anyone. He merely talked informally with people about his philosophical views and tried to get them to think more seriously about their conduct, to make them more aware of the nature of the soul and the pursuit of virtue in their lives.

P: We obviously agree about all that. I thought your first reaction to these recent executions was that it was hard for you to believe that capital punishment is still practiced in civilized societies. My reply is that, statistically speaking, especially when you consider the history of some of the most prominent influential civilizations, the death penalty has been much more the rule than the exception. If it has been resorted to by many peoples in different times and places, one might even say that it is a characteristic feature of civilizations. I've also heard advocates of the death penalty say that it is a necessity of civilization, a way in which to preserve civilized society from degenerating into criminal chaos.

C: Do you really believe that?

P: I think so, but I guess I don't know it with any degree of certainty. I'm honestly not sure what to believe.

C: To me it seems like an extreme and desperate measure on the part of a society to preserve order only when conditions are at their worst rather than a regular feature of normal life in the civilized world. I wouldn't expect it to be a mechanism for maintaining a certain standard of social conduct in a healthy stable civilized society.

P: I can see from your point of view why you would want to say that. Historically, however, it's just not the case. At least in the ancient world, the kinds of societies we think of as prime examples of stable civilizations all practiced capital punishment, and not only in times of temporary emergency and social breakdown. Take ancient Athens again. Did you know that at the Olympic Games married women were not allowed to be spectators? Apparently the reason had something to do with male athletes competing in the nude; unmarried young women, on the other hand, were actually encouraged to attend, possibly as part of their physical education. If a married woman tried to sneak into the games in disguise and was caught, on the other hand, she could be put to death.

C: That doesn't justify it.

P: No, it certainly wouldn't seem to, but it doesn't make it automatically uncivilized either, if by that we mean being in step with practices of the societies we agree to call civilizations.

C: Okay.

P: Here's another example from the same era. Voting in the assembly in ancient Athens was strictly required by law and enforced by the death penalty. You could actually be sentenced to death in the city-state if you were a property-owning free male adult citizen and failed to vote on certain questions that came before the council if you didn't have a very good reason for being absent. I recall a quotation from Euripides' fifth-century B.C.E. tragedy *Hecuba*. He writes, "—Those who take a life—repay it with their own."

C: I remember that. But don't you know the line that follows? It says, "—Justice and the gods exact the loan at last."

P: So?

C: *And the gods.* Not other human beings. The penalty for murder is administered by the gods according to Euripides.

P: Well, it says, "Justice and the gods." Justice is enacted by other human beings and sanctioned by the gods, who ultimately receive the soul of the condemned.

C: I see your point, but I still don't agree.

P: I'm not saying that the death penalty should be lightly imposed. In fact, I think, contrary to the Greeks' freewheeling practice, capital punishment should be applied only in the case of the most extreme crimes and typically in the case of repeat offenders of the same kind of extreme crime.

C: Alright, I get the picture. Let me draw a distinction between a *historical* and a *normative* sense of the word "civilized." When I say that capital punishment is uncivilized—and I still think that it is—I do not mean that historically it wasn't practiced by societies we recognize as civilized but rather that it *ought* not to have been, or that societies we popularly refer to as civilized are not really civilized insofar as they practiced a death penalty.

P: Well, that's very different. If your position now is that the death penalty is uncivilized in the sense that it's morally wrong, then you can't simply rely on precedent or on whatever implications you think might be carried by the use of the words "civilized" and "uncivilized." You can't treat these terms as superlatives or pejoratives for what historically is a fairly widespread institution of law and justice. A strong argument is going to be needed to convince anyone that capital punishment is morally wrong, especially because in the effort to uphold a normative objection to capital punishment, you cannot simply ignore the historical fact that many societies have executed law offenders for one reason or another. If so many societies have had a death penalty, they must have thought there was a moral justification for it, or they wouldn't have been able to sustain it over time.

C: I'm not sure I agree with all of that. There are lots of immoral and unjust practices that have been upheld because they satisfied the interests of powerful rulers or simply because of established precedent and the difficulty of bringing about change in basic social structures. None of these things imply that whatever social practices are in place are therefore morally justified.

P: Fair enough.

C: Anyway, we should look more closely at the attitude toward the death penalty in contemporary societies. If you consider what I would call the majority of enlightened societies in the world today, most of them have decided to outlaw capital punishment on moral grounds. The European Union, for example, has a strict ban on capital punishment and by its charter won't admit any new applicant country for membership in the union if it practices the death penalty.

P: Of course, if you are in sympathy with that position, then you will regard their decision to prohibit capital punishment as evidence that they are taking the moral high ground. I would say that, even if there were no countries anywhere on Earth that permitted capital punishment, that fact by itself would not show from a normative point of view that the death penalty is morally wrong. You cannot decide a philosophical issue simply by adding up the number of persons or countries that do or do not engage in the action at issue. You still need to say why you think it's right or wrong and to offer good arguments for your conclusions. Only then, from the standpoint of a well-argued philosophical justification, can you say, for example, whether the European Union or the United States, Turkey, Japan, and other countries are on the morally right or wrong track in practicing or not practicing a death penalty for certain kinds of crimes.

C: Don't you think it's just inherently barbaric to put people to death? Don't you think it's just obviously morally more advanced for a society not to kill any of its members under any circumstances? I would say that you could plot the social progress a society has made historically in terms of its increasing protection of its citizens and the degree to which it promotes their health and welfare and prevents their unnecessary death. Something similar is true even with respect to a society's treatment of animals. There used to be blood sports in which animals were killed for amusement or worked to death in inhumane ways. As societies have progressed, these practices have been systematically eliminated. Shouldn't this be the case even more so with respect to a society's treatment of human beings? Isn't it undeniable that the positive moral development of a society away from its primitive barbaric beginnings is largely a factor of the extent to which it decreases suffering and death? We no longer accept the idea that prisoners should be tortured in order to obtain confessions, and the U.S. Constitution, which has increasingly become a model with variations for the social contracts of many modern nations, expressly prohibits "cruel and unusual punishment." Doesn't the same moral attitude apply to capital punishment? The more civilized countries ban the death penalty, the more it becomes "unusual" for those countries who continue to execute its prisoners.

P: I see what you mean. And you're right. The Eighth Amendment in the Bill of Rights states, "Excessive bail shall not be required, nor excessive fines imposed, nor cruel and unusual punishments inflicted." You find it ironic or paradoxical, in any case objectionable, that in the United States the highest law of the land should have set a standard of justice for the world that the United States itself seems to be flagrantly violating. I assume that a legal scholar or constitutional historian would argue that the phrase "cruel and unusual punishment" is simply code for the word "torture," which, in a way, is a vague concept. I also think it's worth remarking that the authors of the American Constitution themselves saw no contradiction in prohibiting cruel and unusual punishment at the federal level while at the same time allowing individual states to make provision for a death penalty in the case of certain categories of crimes. That suggests to me that the Constitution distinguishes between cruel and unusual punishment and the death penalty, since otherwise the Constitution would have been interpreted all along as prohibiting capital punishment by any of the individual states for whom the Constitution is the highest law. Would you want to say from your standpoint that if more and more countries decided to reinstate the death penalty, it would then be unobjectionable for the United States to do so too, on the grounds that it was no longer an "unusual" punishment? Why should the administration of justice in the United States depend on what other countries happen to decide is right or wrong for their particular circumstances? Shouldn't Americans have their own independent moral guidelines?

C: Yes, of course. I suppose that the members of every society have an obligation to work these things out for themselves.

P: Then we're right back to the problem of needing to consider good arguments pro or con, for or against the death penalty. We can think about the issue in these terms. First, let's try to decide in the case of our own country whether we think there is any moral justification for continuing the practice of capital punishment in the case of certain kinds of crime. Second, let's see if the reasons we arrive at can be applied generally to any government and any society.

C: Whatever reasons we could have to justify capital punishment or prove that it is unjustified in any particular country ought to hold for any country generally. Or do you think that moral principles are relative to particular times and circumstances?

P: I don't really know what to think about moral relativism or absolutism. I'd prefer to avoid that issue altogether if we possibly could. Let's see how far we can get without entering into that dispute. If there are universal moral principles, we might be able to determine what implications they have for the capital punishment question, and if we get completely stuck or find ourselves in deeper puzzles, we might find it necessary to consider moral value itself in the most general terms rather than merely its applications to culturally relative concrete situations.

C: If we're going to get anywhere on this specific problem, I agree that's probably a good way to proceed. I do not know what to think about moral absolutism versus moral relativism either, and I would rather not start out from any definite assumptions for or against absolute or relative moral value.

P: So, what do you think is so morally objectionable about executing criminals for the kinds of crimes that usually carry that kind of punishment?

C: Well, to begin, going back to the "cruel and unusual punishment" clause in the American Constitution, I would argue that no matter how usual or unusual it is worldwide to execute prisoners, it is always excessively cruel. Capital punishment is morally objectionable to me because it involves the cruel treatment of criminals.

P: What's cruel about it?

C: Are you kidding? Don't you know that persons who have been executed by hanging, firing squad, electrocution, and lethal gas have often taken an extremely long time to die? Sometimes the method fails and people linger on in agony waiting while the apparatus is fixed, or the method of causing death is repeated again and again until it is effective. Do you realize that criminals who are electrocuted have their body hair shaved and are coated with oil to facilitate the passing of electrical current through their skin? And even when it works at its best, this standard method of execution causes extreme pain. Prisoners typically lose control of their bladders and bowels, they experience intensely painful muscle spasms, their eyes pop out, they break their teeth biting down if they are not given a chomp, they have respiratory spasms, and many other kinds of pain. In the case of hanging or death by firing squad or decapitation, the pain and suffering can be even worse. Death by hanging can take as long as twenty minutes when things don't go right, and the same is true when other methods of execution misfire.

P: All that's horrible, of course. I don't think anyone would want to argue that those kinds of occurrences are morally justified, no matter what a convicted criminal has done. As you've described these situations, however, they all sound like accidents or mistakes. They're not intended as part of the punishment. The idea of capital punishment is to execute someone who has committed the sort of crime for which the legal system deems it appropriate for the perpetrator to pay the highest possible penalty.

C: It's still cruel, and I would continue to say that it's a barbaric, uncivilized way to treat even our worst law offenders.

P: Really? I mean, do you know what some of these people have done?

C: Yes, I think I do.

P: Because when you think about the monstrous disregard for life and suffering that some of these criminals have been found guilty of committing, it's hard to regard them in turn with any level of sympathy. We are talking about persons who have ruthlessly murdered, raped, and tortured other human beings. Some of these criminals have killed repeatedly and in the most horrible ways imaginable, causing prolonged pain and misery to their victims, brutally cutting short the lives of persons who might have enjoyed many years of happiness with their families while making important contributions to society. And this is not to mention the loss to the friends and loved ones of the individuals whom capital offense criminals have wronged.

C: I'm aware of that. There's a part of me that emotionally cries out for vengeance against those kinds of criminals of an eye-for-an-eye and tooth-for-a-tooth sort. I sometimes think that whatever monstrous things a criminal has done to someone else should be done to them. Is that what people mean when they say the punishment should fit the crime? When I consider justice as unemotionally as I can, however, I once again find myself thinking that it's a hallmark of any civilized and morally decent society to resist those urges and not allow ourselves as a law-abiding people to sink to the level of the worst criminal elements in society. If we do, then we're morally no better than the criminals we prosecute, imprison, and in other ways punish. We must avoid reacting emotionally to these kinds of crimes and adopt a public policy based on the rational requirements of ethics and justice.

P: I'm glad to hear you say that because I think that's precisely why the death penalty should never be eliminated as a punishment for the worst sorts of crimes.

C: I can't agree, not unless you can convince me that capital punishment is morally justifiable. And that's not going to be easy. Two wrongs never make a right, you know.

P: That's just more sloganeering. It's like labeling an action as uncivilized without providing anything more than polemics and propaganda for a controversial moral stance. I might even admit that two wrongs don't make a right, but of course the whole question here is whether capital punishment is in fact morally wrong. If it is, then it shouldn't be practiced, period, regardless of whether it is applied only in the case of the most heinous crimes, as you would say, of the greatest wrongs. But that's just the point at issue. Is capital punishment in fact immoral, is it a wrong, or can it be right to execute criminals under certain situations? If the latter is true, then it's not a question of anyone trying to make two wrongs into a right, whatever that old cliché is finally understood.

C: Don't evade the question. I said that capital punishment is always at least potentially cruel and hence that it ought to be excluded by the same moral considerations that properly moved the framers of the American Constitution to prohibit cruel and unusual punishments anywhere within the legal system. It is morally wrong, there is no other way to put it, and there's nothing cliché about the idea to treat another human being, regardless of what he or she has done or believed and convicted by a court of law as having done, with the kind of cruelty that is represented by and is always potentially a result of capital punishment.

P: Well, I don't think I've lost sight of your point. But I urge you also to remember what I said, which is that it need not be the purpose of capital punishment to cause excessive pain. It should at most be only an accidental occurrence that happens when things go wrong and the equipment through no one's deliberate fault happens to malfunction. That kind of thing occurs in many areas of life, in which it would be absurd to suppose that we would therefore prohibit the activity. Take dentistry or other medical procedures, for example. Some of these cause significant pain, particularly when things accidentally go wrong. We would not forbid the practice of dentistry just because sometimes a drill slips and hurts a patient, causing unnecessary suffering, or when the wrong kidney is removed in surgery through sheer bad luck during a complicated operation. Even where gross incompetence is at fault, I would say we should target the incompetence, not prohibit the practice. I could give a hundred similar examples without too much difficulty, the conclusion of which would be the same in every case. The mere potential for things to go wrong and for a criminal to suffer an unpleasant execution by itself doesn't seem like a strong enough reason to prohibit capital punishment, especially if there are good independent reasons to justify its practice.

C: I agree, again. But I think that there's another kind of cruelty built into the death penalty that makes it inherently immoral, even when everything goes right, so to speak, and the execution equipment functions as its supposed to and brings about a quick and painless death.

P: Is that so? Because I was going to remind you that in most states in the United States these days execution is performed by lethal injection, which appears to be quick, effective, and painless. Are you familiar with the method?

C: Yes I am. Three fluids are injected successively through an intravenous needle. The prisoner is strapped with padding onto a table and is first put to sleep by a general anesthetic, specifically, sodium thiopental. Then a second trickle of fluid, pancuronium bromide, is added to the flow that causes the lungs to stop pumping, and finally a poison, potassium chloride, enters the bloodstream that goes directly to the heart and causes it to stop beating so that the person dies painlessly in an unconscious state. It's all very clinical and antiseptic, and, in my opinion, no less morally unjustified for all that.

P: Somebody got an A in chemistry.

C: I was just reading about it.

P: I would think that such a method of execution answers all the moral objections you could possibly have against it. Have you ever had general anesthetic? You are pricked with a needle, no worse than getting a flu shot, and in a matter of just a few seconds you are oblivious to all sensation, in a very deep state of unconsciousness. I had some minor surgery last year for which I was given general anesthesia, and it was completely painless. I can't remember anything happening, and I never felt the scalpel when my skin was cut or anything that happened while I was under. It was just as though I didn't exist at the time. What's more, if something had gone wrong while I was being operated on, if I'd have had an allergic reaction to the anesthesia or if the surgery had somehow failed and I had died on the operating table, as happens every day to some people, I simply would have never woken up. I would have died peacefully in a state of no pain or awareness of what was happening to me. I would have just disappeared from among the living, at least as a biologically embodied consciousness. And that's the way I ordinarily think of myself existing as a person.

C: Right. If there's an immortal soul that survives on the other side of death, that's an entirely different question. We're only asking about the morality or immorality of the death penalty as a practice among the living that results in death. Whatever, if anything happens to the soul thereafter, if there is such a thing, is something else again, something, I would say, that we don't know anything about anyway.

P: I'm with you there. Let's leave religion and philosophical questions about the soul and its mortality or immortality out of things, if we can. So what objection can you possibly have to the death penalty, provided that it's performed mercifully by means of something like lethal injection? What's cruel about capital punishment if the execution is performed painlessly and, I would say, with more solemnity and dignity than most of those who are punished for capital offenses typically deserve?

C: Ah, you see, your last remark suggests part of the deeper disagreement that divides us. You seem to think that dignity is a matter of *desert*, that people have to deserve to be treated with dignity, whereas I would say it is unconditional, even for persons who have committed truly egregious moral offenses. I would insist that all persons, simply by virtue of being persons, have moral rights that must always be respected and that there is something necessarily morally wrong about the death penalty because it refuses by its very nature to acknowledge the intrinsic moral worth of any and every human being. To take another person's life for any reason or under any circumstances, regardless of how painless the method, violates respect for the individual's moral personhood. Many criminals have no regard for the right to life of others, but that does not justify its total disregard by the members of a civilized community. It is especially incumbent on a just society not to violate the respect for moral rights of every person, especially when a law offender by harming or killing others has acted in disregard and disrespect for their inalienable moral value as persons and, in particular, their right to life.

P: The question of whether moral rights are absolutely unconditional or can be forfeited as a result of certain kinds of behavior toward others, is, I suspect you're correct, going to be one of the principal issues that separates us. Although, by the way, I also believe that the recognition and protection of moral rights is highly important in individual morality and social policy. So perhaps we should reserve detailed consideration of that part of our discussion until later, when we have looked into all other relevant aspects of the question. If we can come to some kind of agreement before we reach that difficulty, then we might be able to save ourselves some complicated investigations that might never reach a satisfactory resolution anyway. If we can spare ourselves the trouble and still achieve agreement about the ethics of capital punishment, then we owe it to ourselves to try to do so. That's what I recommend, anyway. What do you think?

C: I agree. And I still think there is inherent cruelty, questions of moral dignity and respect for persons aside, in the systematic execution of criminals, even by lethal injection, if that turns out to be the most painless effective method of causing someone to die.

P: Well, then, what do you mean by cruelty? What is it for someone to be treated cruelly?

C: There are physical or bodily as well as psychological kinds of cruelty.

P: But what is cruelty generally? I can tell you easily what I mean by the word. To act cruelly is to take pleasure in the deliberate infliction of pain, whether it is, as you say, physical or psychological.

C: I'm not sure I understand the distinction.

P: Well, when a doctor causes pain, for example, in resetting a bone that has gotten out of joint or in performing a physically intrusive examination, I would not say that the doctor is being cruel because the doctor takes no pleasure in causing the pain and is performing the act in question for the purpose of trying to benefit rather than harm the patient. If, however, the doctor did precisely the same things, engaged in precisely the same actions, purely for the sake of hurting the patient, without regard for the patient's well-being, and in order to enjoy the suffering of another, then the action would be cruel. It is not so much the actual physical movements that make the deed cruel, if, as I suggest, these could be exactly the same in both cases. What makes the difference is the attitude of the person who inflicts the pain and the purpose for which the pain is inflicted.

C: So, you think that someone has to enjoy the suffering of another person in order for the action that causes the pain to be cruel?

P: Absolutely.

C: Well, I'm not sure I agree even with that. But if I did, I might just substitute another word for "cruel" and "cruelty" in order to convey what

I'm trying to say. Perhaps taking pleasure in the deliberate infliction of medically unjustified pain, of causing pain simply for the sake of causing pain, is a sufficient but not necessary condition for being cruel. The reason why I find capital punishment morally objectionable remains the same even when it is accomplished in a supposedly humane and painless way for whoever is executed.

P: What don't you like about my distinction?

C: I don't think in the first place that it accords very well with the way we actually talk about cruelty and cruel actions. I don't believe that we are necessarily speaking inexactly or metaphorically when we say, for example, that nature is often cruel to the weak and injured in the animal kingdom or when we refer to a cruel winter or a cruel fate or a cruel turn of events. These occurrences need not involve anyone taking pleasure in suffering at all; they are cruel just because they produce suffering pure and simple. I might even speak of a morally upright physician as performing a cruel procedure if it causes pain, regardless of whether the physician takes pleasure in the pain a patient suffers. In other words, I am not sure by any criterion of received linguistic usage that cruelty requires the kind of sadistic attitude you have described. Furthermore, I don't think that this is anything like the sense of the word "cruel" that the authors of the American Constitution had in mind when they explicitly prohibited cruel and unusual punishments. Would they have been satisfied for criminals to be painfully tortured, provided that no one involved in the process happened to experience any twisted pleasure in the infliction of pain that a victim was made to suffer? I don't really think so, do you?

P: No, I guess not.

C: I believe it makes no difference at all whether an executioner experiences pleasure or satisfaction or is emotionally indifferent, bored, or even inwardly horrified and repulsed by causing another person to die. The same goes for anyone else involved in the judicial proceedings that ultimately result in the execution of a criminal. Perhaps the judge enjoys sentencing a person to death, or perhaps the judge is totally repelled by the prospect, renounces the suffering that the individual might suffer in the process, but feels compelled by the requirements of the law to impose such a sentence in the case of certain kinds of crime. It really doesn't matter, and it shouldn't matter. In a way, the question is, What does the sentencing to death and carrying out of the death sentence mean or represent? What are we saying as a society when we have embodied in our laws and social practices the possibility of ending a person's life as a penalty for something an individual has done? If cruelty is a matter of the attitude that those involved have, or their intentions or purpose when they cause another person to be executed, then what I have called the inherent cruelty of capital punishment may after all be irrelevant.

P: Well, that's certainly what I was thinking. And that's the direction I was trying to take the discussion. Because I don't imagine that cruelty in the sense of sadistic pleasure in the sufferings of another is necessarily a part of legal executions. To whatever extent cruelty so defined might be in the thoughts of persons involved in the penal system, they could take pleasure even in another person's imprisonment or any other type of punishment that falls short of execution. And I don't imagine it would be reasonable to suppose that the authors of the U.S. Constitution merely wanted to prohibit only those punishments for which any of the persons responsible might experience a secret joy or pleasure in the sufferings of someone being punished.

C: Very good. So, let's move along in this way. Let's just exclude questions of cruelty in the sense of experiencing pleasure in the pain suffered by others. If you want, I'll simply give you the word "cruelty" to think of and define however you like. What I am talking about when I say that I think capital punishment is inherently immoral can then be better expressed by saying only that I believe what is wrong about the death penalty is that it involves a degree and kind of suffering that is incompatible with the moral values of a just society.

P: Why? You've already admitted that physical pain is eliminable as a factor in the most humane method of execution. Death by lethal injection is quick and painless. Now you've ruled out cruelty as essential to the problem of capital punishment by admitting that the attitudes and intentions of those who sentence and carry out a death sentence are irrelevant to the ethics of the most extreme form of criminal justice. So, what is left as a possible objection?

C: There is the psychological suffering of knowing that one is to be killed at a certain time and place.

P: We all have to die, at some time and some place or other.

C: But a condemned man or woman knows in advance when this is going to happen. And this creates a kind of psychological suffering that is unlike any other punishment prescribed by law.

P: Is that really so different, or so special, as to make capital punishment morally objectionable on grounds of cruelty or suffering?

C: The great nineteenth-century Russian novelist Fyodor Dostoyevsky described it as the worst imaginable penalty. And he should know because he was sentenced to death by the government of the czar of Russia for his part in owning a printing press that was used to publish revolutionary socialist pamphlets calling for the overthrow of the monarchy and the liberation of the serfs. Dostoyevsky makes this observation based on his personal experience in several of his major writings, including the novel *Crime and Punishment*, and in his earlier partly autobiographical work *The City of the Dead*. Dostoyevsky says that the absolutely worst part of the death sentence—and the part that makes it inescapably an unusual punishment, no matter how many cultures continue to practice it—is that the sentenced person unlike anyone else in any other walk of life knows the exact time, place, and circumstance of his or her death and can therefore anticipate its occurrence in time with each passing moment leading to the execution.

P: Well, wait a minute. Dostoyevsky wasn't actually executed, was he?

C: No. He was reprieved at the last moment when he was already blindfolded and facing a firing squad. The trauma of coming so close to the fatal moment brought on the epilepsy with which he was plagued for the rest of his life.

P: Let me get this straight. Dostoyevsky was not actually executed, right? So he didn't actually *know* in advance when and where he was going to die. He *believed* that he was going to be executed, and he *thought he knew* when and where it was to occur, but as a matter of fact, he didn't know. He had good reason to believe that he would be executed on the date set for his execution, but as things turned out he was mistaken. He was wrong in such a way, moreover, that it seems natural to say he didn't know and wasn't in a position to know whether it is an immoral source of suffering for a condemned person to know that they are in fact to be executed at a certain time in a certain place and in a certain way. Isn't that so? Because he didn't know at all.

C: Oh, come on. I mean, the fact that at the last minute he was reprieved doesn't change anything. He could just as easily have been executed were it not for a decision on the part of the authorities that was completely out of his control. The psychological suffering he experienced was the same up until that moment, believing that he was about to die, as if he had in fact been killed. So not only was he in a unique position to know what it feels like to be condemned to death, but as things turned out he lived in order to be able to think and write about it.

P: I don't know . . . I think that since he wasn't actually executed, it proves he didn't really *know* when he was going to die. And I would say the same about anyone else in that situation. There are innumerable things that might intervene to prevent someone from actually being executed in the end, no matter how convinced they are that the sentence is going to be carried out. A pardon could come, in the United States, for example, from a governor or the president, at the last minute. Or there could be a political coup or a prison riot, or any number of other things could happen to prevent the death sentence from actually being carried out.

C: How likely is that?

P: Well, as you've admitted, it happened in Dostoyevsky's case. The mere possibility is enough to hold out a ray of hope for persons who are condemned to prevent them from lapsing into total despair. Their situation is not necessarily different from persons who are told by their doctor that they have only a few days or weeks or months to live. The condemned can still expect a miracle, knowing that it's happened to others, even while they are being led to the execution chamber, and that might be enough to preserve them from undue psychological suffering.

C: Dostoyevsky's is a particularly instructive case because most people today would regard the crime for which he was sentenced as nothing more than the inoffensive exercise of the right of free speech.

P: I suppose it was interpreted as conspiracy in an act of high treason, which has been regarded as an offense deserving the death penalty in many political contexts. Still, I would say on the contrary that Dostoyevsky's example proves nothing of philosophical interest at all.

C: Why in the world not?

P: Because it all goes back to individual psychology again. It is like the question of whether someone involved in the sentencing or execution of capital punishment takes a sadistic pleasure in the sufferings of the condemned. What difference does it make? The fact is that such psychological experiences are highly subjective, a matter of individual personality and outlook. Okay, so Dostoyevsky with his particular personality found it highly disturbing to know in advance when he might die. It certainly doesn't follow that everyone would have the same reaction. It might not bother some types at all, who might simply not care. I would say that this is even likely in the case of certain hard types who have become inured to the value of life and may have completely lost interest even in their own future welfare. They might even take comfort in having the greatest object of uncertainty removed from their thinking. Dostoyevsky had a lot to lose, and so he naturally looked forward to a definite termination to his life with deep regret and terrible anticipation. And he presumably believed that he was acting rightly to oppose the social-economic abuses of the Russian czar, so he must have thought that his death sentence was morally unjustified. Besides, he was a person of sensitive poetic intellectual temperament, a borderline epileptic, as you have acknowledged, who is likely to have been more deeply affected by morbidly dwelling on the upcoming occasion of his scheduled execution. There is no special reason to think that everyone who is sentenced to death would think in the same way about the approaching deadline—if I can use that term with no pun intended and without appearing to make light of the situation. I can even imagine that some personality types would find it consoling to know in advance exactly when and where they are to die because it would give a kind of closure to their expectations, a terminus to their imprisonment, and a limit within which they can order their affairs and put their lives in perspective. The rest of us as a rule don't have such an opportunity, and there are advantages and disadvantages to everything in life, including the circumstances of one's death. In a way it is good not to know, and in another way it might be good to know, and it need not produce undue suffering or even cruel suffering to know in advance when one is to die.

C: I agree with Dostoyevsky. I would hate to know when I am going to live my last day, to count down the days and minutes until the whole machinery of the law comes into play and one is lead away to die, even if it is done by means of a completely painless method of execution.

P: Well, it is after all supposed to be a punishment. The question is whether capital punishment is immoral or morally prohibited by higher principles of ethics and justice. Don't you think you would feel differently about it all if you had done something truly horrible to another person and were receiving the punishment your actions had merited?

C: I don't know. I'm feeling rather at the limit of my imagination. I can't imagine in the first place what it would be like to commit any of the sorts of crimes for which capital punishments are prescribed in the few countries that still have the death penalty. Let alone can I imagine what it would be like to stand trial for such an offense, go through the appeals process, spend the better part of a decade in prison, and then take the final walk to an execution chamber.

P: That's for sure. I can't imagine being in that situation either. Thank goodness. What I *can* imagine is being falsely accused and sentenced, winding up on the wrong side of the law purely as a result of mistaken identity or by being framed. That kind of thing. Of course, under those circumstances, I wouldn't feel that I was being punished for anything I had done. It would be a personal tragedy for me and people who know me, but it wouldn't be the same as if I had acted so wrongly that in my heart I accepted the fact that I deserved to pay the ultimate penalty.

C: You see, that's part of my point. The fact that there is a death penalty means that some people can be wrongly sentenced to death, and that's a punishment for which there is no correction or reversal once the sentence is carried out. We can't fix things or make them right if there's been a mistake in the case of capital punishment. There's always a possibility, even when all persons concerned are acting with the best of intentions, for justice to miscarry. As long as the penalty incurred is less than death, then something can always be done to redress the wrong and compensate those who have been punished in error. What we cannot do in any case is bring someone back from the dead once they have been executed; it's as permanent a punishment as there can be.

P: That's true. However, I'm not sure to what extent the same problem doesn't affect the imperfect prosecution of justice generally. What should we think about the outcome of events when someone is wrongly sentenced to life imprisonment and dies of natural causes while in prison? That situation can't be fixed or redressed either. For that matter, even if the person does not die while in prison and is discovered to be innocent of the charges for which he or she was sentenced, we cannot give back to that person the time or life experiences that he or she has wrongfully had taken away. Persons who have been falsely imprisoned will typically have missed out on unrepeatable events, lost their jobs, had their careers ruined, been deprived of their houses, destroyed their marriages, been separated from their children, and all other prospects for a normal, happy life. Even if we try afterward to compensate them for some of these losses, we cannot hope to restore what has been taken away from them, just as unfortunately we cannot bring back to life a person who has been mistakenly executed through a miscarriage of justice. That is regrettable in the extreme, needless to say. But there are many regrettable aspects of life generally and the conduct of justice in particular.

C: So, that's a risk *you're* prepared to take, eh? You see, this is exactly why I say that capital punishment is morally insupportable—because its bad effects cannot be recompensed in any way, at least not for the person most directly affected.

P: Again, except as a matter of degree, I don't see that much difference between malfunctions of justice in the case of capital punishment and those of conventional punishments on a spectrum of situations that includes falsely imprisoned persons who die of natural causes while incarcerated.

C: There's a huge difference between not being able to adequately compensate a person who's still alive for a mistaken sentencing and someone who can't be compensated at all because he or she has been mistakenly executed. I think you're being awfully callous about an individual losing his or her life through a mistaken judgment in a court of law.

P: Not at all. I agree that this would be a terrible misfortune and that we should make every effort to prevent wrong verdicts from happening. That is why there exists a complex system of checks and balances and opportunities to discover mistakes within the justice system before a death sentence is actually carried out. There are regular appeals and judicial reviews of court proceedings and sentencing, all of which generally occur after a fair trial in which the accused at least in the United States has a court appointed lawyer if he or she cannot afford one. The accused is tried in a context of scientific evaluation of material data and examination and cross-examination of witnesses in an adversarial dialectic of prosecution and defense with definite rules of evidence and fair procedures of advocacy and argument. A judge or jury decides whether a person is guilty of a crime for which capital punishments can be adjudicated, and there are frequent opportunities for attorneys to qualify the sentencing for such crimes in defense of their clients' interests. As a rule, in judicial proceedings as they actually occur, it is only the most heinous repeat offenders of the most horrendous crimes in which guilt is clearly established with no mitigating factors who actually receive a sentence of death.

C: It sounds like you're a confirmed advocate of the status quo.

P: As a matter of fact, I've got serious reservations about the American judiciary system. Nevertheless, when it comes to the procedures and judicial review involved in capital punishment cases, although I recognize that it is always possible for mistakes to be made, I think that with refinements and adjustments that might be instituted for improving the process, on the whole the mechanism is fair, perhaps about as fair as one could imagine any such fallible practical human enterprise being.

C: Yes? But if it's fallible, as you acknowledge, then why not err on the side of caution and refuse to perpetuate a category of punishments for which there cannot even in principle be a solution when things go wrong? We know, if we are reasonable, that sometimes mistakes are bound to be made. So why not avoid the possibility of a personal catastrophe from occurring if we can prevent it by simply doing away with the death penalty? Since there is an alternative, why not limit punishments in the case of the worst law offenders to life imprisonment, say, without possibility of parole? Why wouldn't that serve the interests of justice as well as or even better than the execution of criminals?

P: That, I'm afraid, is going to be a rather long story. Maybe we should reserve that discussion for another occasion when we have the time to consider the arguments in detail.

C: I'll look forward to that.

P: Let's do it tomorrow, if you're free. I'd like nothing better, and I think I owe you a full explanation. In the meantime, I'm sure you can imagine from what I've said so far not only that I regard capital punishment as defensible from the kinds of objections you've been raising but also that there are positive reasons why the death penalty ought to remain as a category of punishment for the worst kinds of crimes. Otherwise, I'd just agree with you that life in prison should be the maximum penalty. As it is, I think not only that the objections to capital punishment can be answered, but that there are very good reasons for preserving the death penalty as an option in sentencing—positive justifications, as well as sound replies to criticisms—provided that there are adequate checks and balances and judicial review at every stage of the process.

C: Well, I don't know that you're going to be able to persuade me. I think that from a logical point of view, capital punishment cannot possibly be morally justified. It cannot be supported on ethical grounds, if I'm right.

P: Why not?

C: I would say that the only possible moral justification for a punishment is to improve someone's behavior. If a child misbehaves, we are morally justified in administering a minor punishment in order to correct the child and impress on his or her memory the need to think and act differently. There is no justification for simply causing a child pain or restricting the child's freedom or inflicting any other kind of punishment except to benefit the child by instruction with respect to future behavior. The same is true, I would argue, with respect to the punishment of adults who have broken the law. We can only morally justify punishing them as a way of adjusting their behavior and bringing them into line with the social expectations of responsible action. Otherwise, all we are doing is causing harm to another person with no higher purpose in view and no greater benefit for the person who is punished. We cannot morally justify punishment for its own sake, punishment for the sake of punishment, as some people speak of art for art's sake. In the case of execution, which I would say is really just legalized murder, the situation is very different. If a person is put to death, then there is no possibility of that kind of "punishment" serving to improve or correct their behavior in the future because in the nature of the case the condemned has no future and hence no possibility to correct his or her behavior in response to the punishment—if "punishment" is what we still want to call it. I suppose I'd be willing to speak of capital punishment as a punishment in the proper sense of the word, but for the reasons I just mentioned I would argue that the death penalty cannot possibly be morally justified as a punishment.

P: Oh? Well, if you really believe that, then shouldn't you also reject life imprisonment without the possibility of parole as a morally unjustifiable punishment? There too the nature of the sentence precludes a person's reforming their social behavior.

C: Not at all. A convict in prison is still living in a special subsociety, a subculture within the prison, and has countless opportunities to interact with fellow prisoners in an ethically correct or incorrect way. Some lifetime prisoners never learn their lesson and continue to commit crimes even while in prison, but others respond positively to the punishment and live out the rest of their lives in prison in a morally upright way, abiding by the rules and respecting the rights of others. Through various channels, they can also have a positive impact on the world outside of prison if they get themselves straightened out and reform their behavior by getting control of their actions at some point during their incarceration.

P: Maybe, sure. But that's also true of persons condemned to the death penalty before the sentence is actually carried out. And, as you point out, part of the punishment, as Dostoyevsky says, is knowing the length of time one has left to live, to have an opportunity to reflect on the severity of the crimes committed, and to acknowledge their guilt, at least to themselves, and perhaps modify their behavior at least during the years and months and weeks and days that remain to them. How is that different from the situation of a person who is sentenced to life in prison without the possibility of parole and who also someday dies of natural causes while still in prison? I imagine that you'll say the case of capital punishment is different because the sentence is not fully carried out until the prisoner is actually executed, so whatever change of heart or conduct the person undergoes as a result of being under sentence does not count as a morally justifiable result of the punishment. I would reply that the very same thing is true in the case of the punishment of life in prison without the possibility of parole. That sentence too is not actually complete, not actually carried out, until the person dies of natural causes or, regrettably, perhaps, as a result of an act of violence, within the prison. Only then can we say that the punishment is fulfilled, that the person has actually been subjected to life imprisonment without the possibility of parole. In that case, it's equally true for logical reasons that the person never has an opportunity to apply the lessons of the completed punishment to future conduct.

C: That's not what I was going to say. The problem I see is that the sentence of life imprisonment is actually carried out from the first moment the prisoner begins serving the sentence, regardless of how long thereafter he or she continues to live. A death sentence isn't carried out at all or in any degree unless or until the prisoner is actually executed, at which point it is logically too late for any morally redeeming effect of the punishment to take place in transforming the prisoner's life in a positive way, even if it is only for the rest of his or her life in prison. Until that point in the case of capital punishment, the condemned person is not undergoing the sentence but awaiting it, counting the days and hours before it takes place. Capital punishment is different in this regard precisely because it begins as it ends only with the death of the prisoner, whereupon, as I've urged, no possibility exists for the person to learn from or benefit from the event. As I see things, therefore, there is no logical possibility for the death penalty to be morally justified as a punishment.

P: I'm beginning to understand what you're saying . . .

C: So, are you also beginning to agree that capital punishment cannot possibly be morally justified as a punishment?

P: I don't think so. The reason is that I'm not sure, you haven't yet convinced me, that the only moral justification for any type of punishment must be the intention to bring about a positive change in a person's behavior. That might be how we try to justify certain kinds of punishments, by analogy with the little punishments we give to children to correct their future behavior for their own good. Why suppose that's the only moral justification for punishing someone, especially in the case of morally responsible adults who presumably already know the difference between right and wrong and have deliberately chosen in some cases to do terribly wrong things? Adults who are sentenced to death for serious crimes are not still in need of training or moral education in the way that children are. So, why should we expect the moral justification for punishing adults to be the same as or even analogous to the reasons we have for punishing children when they act wrongly?

C: Well, what do you think the moral justification for punishing adults is supposed to be? What kind of moral justification can there be for capital punishment, in which the condemned person is annihilated when the sentence is carried out? What are we supposed to have accomplished by killing a capital crimes offender that could morally justify that kind of punishment?

P: There are other ways of thinking about moral justification besides producing a positive benefit for the person directly and immediately affected by an action, in this case the person being punished.

C: Don't forget that we have set aside considerations about the immortality of the soul. So you can't appeal to the idea some people have accepted, that a death sentence might benefit a person's immortal soul by purifying it of its crime for an improved existence in an afterlife.

P: I wouldn't dream of offering that kind of argument. The Inquisition in the late medieval world apparently tried to justify the use of torture and death for the good of the immortal souls of persons who were often falsely made to confess to various kinds of heresies against the Church. That whole way of thinking is completely repugnant to me, and I couldn't consider anything similar as a moral justification of the death penalty even if I believed that the soul is immortal and survives intact as a distinct personality with memories and expectations after the body's death.

C: Then what kind of moral justification for capital punishment do you have in mind?

P: Capital punishment is not intended to correct or improve the behavior of the condemned person; that is not what justifies it on moral grounds. It is rather a payment, a penalty, a fine, so to speak, of the highest sort, in which the guilty person pays the greatest possible price for the most socially unacceptable kinds of actions.

C: Do you mean like a parking ticket or a library fine?

P: That way of describing it makes it seem trivial, but, in principle, yes, that's roughly the kind of thing I mean.

C: Well, that interpretation of the rationale for capital punishment is not going to help your cause. After all, what is the moral justification of library fines and parking tickets if not to affect and influence the behavior of library patrons and motorists, providing them with an incentive not to keep books out longer than they're supposed to or to park where it's illegal to park or for longer than they've paid to park? The point of instituting fines and penalties in that sense is all future-directed in just the way we've already agreed is impossible in the case of the death penalty.

P: Are you absolutely sure that all penalties are meant to influence future behavior? I agree that some of them are, just as I agree that some punishments are designed to improve the way people act. The question is whether this is always or essentially true or whether there are also some kinds of punishments and penalties that don't have this characteristic or, I would say, this limitation.

Similarly in the case of fines. Suppose that I have misbehaved in my profession, say, as a physician, committing acts that make me guilty of medical malpractice. For the sake of example, suppose that I have written prescriptions for drugs that patients did not really need for any sound medical reason but that they just wanted to use for fun. If I am caught and convicted, then I might very properly have my medical license revoked and be forbidden by a court of law from practicing medicine, and I might also be fined as a penalty in punishment for what I did.

There are many similar examples that we could also give, all with the same implication, that the penalty, in this case a monetary fine, is not meant to influence my future behavior, since we are assuming that after I have lost my license it will no longer be possible for me to practice medicine or write prescriptions for drugs. The penalty is merely a punishment, making me pay, in this case, for my hypothetical unprofessional misbehavior. By doing so, I am made to recognize that I have acted wrongly, and the punishment makes this meaningful and real. Also, the revoking of my license to practice medicine if I am found guilty of medical malpractice puts a definite end to my being able to act wrongly in the same way ever again.

In the situations I am imagining, a person who has done something wrong simply deserves to pay a price for having done so, under the law or at the discretion of a judge or jury. I think this kind of thing happens very often in the administration of justice. It is common for a penalty to be exacted independently of whether doing so will have any positive or beneficial effect on the future behavior of the person who is made to pay. I would say that this is what morally justifies imprisonment for any length of time as a punishment for less than capital offenses, even when there is no prospect for or attempt made at rehabilitating a prisoner. The convicted person has done something wrong and is expected to pay a price for his or her wrongdoing.

A morally justifiable judicial practice makes the penalty paid appropriate in cost and severity to the crime. If I keep my book out too late from the library, I may need to pay a few cents to a dollar or so per day for my offense since I am making the book unavailable in the meantime to others who may want to read it. It is what I owe to the library for breaking the rule. And this would be true, I would say, even if, for example, I were to go blind in the meantime or for some other reason would never have any reason to check out another book. The same is true of my parking violations. If I overpark or park in a restricted space, then I owe a penalty for doing so, a higher penalty, typically, than a library fine, of ten or fifteen or twenty dollars, depending on the circumstances, even if I were incapacitated from driving ever again in the future or even if another part of the penalty were to permanently deprive me of my driving license. In many cases, the modification of future behavior, particularly for the benefit of the rule breaker or lawbreaker, is logically irrelevant to the moral justification of the penalty or punishment applied.

Now, on a scale in which the fine or penalty is made proportionately appropriate to the offense, we might say that from library fines to parking tickets to thefts, rapes, manslaughter, or killings undertaken in the heat of passion to cold-blooded calculated murder, treason, or other high crimes, the fine or penalty is and morally should be proportionally higher, and in the worst cases involving the worst crimes, for persons defended in a court of law but found guilty, their convictions sustained on appeal, and so on, they might be required to pay the greatest penalty, or "fine," so to speak, by forfeiting their own lives. If you're late returning your book, you may owe twenty-five cents, even if you are never able to take out a book again; if you are a physician and you write drug prescriptions for the wrong reason, you may lose your license to practice medicine and pay tens or even hundreds of thousands of dollars as a fitting punishment for what you have done. If with malice and premeditation under aggravating circumstances you take another person's life, then you may need to pay for the crime by forfeiting your own life, even if the nature of the penalty in that case is such that you are thereby prevented from learning from the punishment and improving your social behavior in the future. If you take a life, you might owe the loss of your own life in return. And that is justice, what the principles of law in a just society require.

C: I think we could question even whether library fines or parking tickets were justified in the circumstances you've described . . .

P: Wouldn't you be required to pay a traffic ticket you've incurred even if you were never able to drive again in the future? That is the legal and, I would say, morally justified penalty for something you've done in the past, breaking a rule or a certain law. It doesn't matter what you might or might not be able to do in the future, which makes the punishment logically independent of any moral justification the payment of the penalty or fine might have for your later conduct.

C: Alright. That's fair enough, although I am not convinced about the analogy between these lesser infractions and the penalties they are assigned and capital punishment. The difference in degree of crime and penalty is so great that I am unsure that it does not simply amount to a difference in kind and that we cannot reasonably draw inferences from the justification for fines and penalties in lesser cases to the extreme case of capital punishment. I think that in all those less-than-capital cases the moral justification for the penalty is not necessarily to influence the behavior of the wrongdoer but to serve as a check, reminder, and correction for the conduct of others. It works, in other words, to sustain an entire social institution in which penalties are ultimately justified by the overall effect they have on controlling social behavior, so that it is better on the whole not to tolerate exceptions in unusual circumstances but to require every individual to pay the penalty even if his or her particular behavior cannot be positively or beneficially affected by their meeting the requirements of a general rule or principle of law.

P: That, of course, is more grist to my mill. Because I would say that the existence of the death penalty serves as a positive deterrent to persons who might otherwise be inclined to violate the social contract by committing the most grievous offenses like premeditated murder.

C: I thought we might eventually get around to this topic. Do you realize that you're on especially weak ground there? The scientific sociological evidence all points to the opposite conclusion, that the death penalty either makes no difference in the number of murders, for example, or actually increases the number of capital crimes.

P: How can that be? I would have thought that the existence of the death penalty would provide the strongest imaginable reason for persons who generally love life to avoid committing the kinds of crimes that carry the possibility of execution.

C: In some ways that's a reasonable assumption. The trouble is that for complicated reasons most serious crimes are not prevented by the possibility of capital punishment. Even in the case of premeditated murder, most perpetrators act without regard for those kinds of consequences. Possibly they are living in denial about what might happen to them, even concerning the likelihood of their getting caught or being found guilty. Others may simply not care because in their own minds they believe themselves to be justified in what they are doing. They think that they have suffered unfairly at the hands of their intended victims or believe that they have incurred some other kind of wrong, for which an act of murder, if that's the kind of case we're thinking of, would put things right in the world and which they believe as a result is something they are entitled to do. For criminals of that type, whatever penalty society might impose, they might convince themselves it would be worth it in order to accomplish their purposes, even if they believe it is likely that they will eventually have to pay the ultimate penalty.

P: I don't think I understand that. Are you saying, if you agree with my previous analogy, that having a stiff fine doesn't deter borrowers from returning their books late? I know that in my own case, if there weren't a fine, a penalty or punishment, I wouldn't concern myself with whether I brought my books back on time. It just wouldn't matter to me because there would be no incentive to follow the rules. Isn't it just the same in society at large with respect to prohibitions against murder, kidnapping and other acts of severe violence, treason, and the like? I would certainly think twice and then think twice again before committing an action that carried such a heavy penalty as the possibility of being executed for my crime.

C: Maybe so, but that's not what the statistics and the expert studies have concluded.

P: I can't believe it. I still can't believe that in a number of cases knowing in advance that one might be executed for committing a crime like murder wouldn't provide a good reason for someone rationally considering whether to take another person's life to think twice about it and restrain themselves from giving in to the impulse to take revenge in that extreme way. What about crimes in which profit is the motive? What about persons who are considering murder in order to collect insurance on a relative or in order to take someone else's job or property? You can't enjoy the fruits of that kind of crime if you are executed. So, if your reason for thinking of doing it is in order to attain some kind of material gain, it would simply be irrational to make murder part of your plan, knowing in advance that you thereby risk a death sentence. If you put that kind of consideration together with the common knowledge that modern scientific criminal forensics makes it extremely difficult to commit any type of crime and not be discovered and punished, the combined force of those considerations must surely provide a strong deterrent for anyone thinking of committing a capital crime for the sake of profit.

C: It's a good theory. But the statistics don't bear it out. The facts seem to be otherwise, comparing societies that have the death penalty versus those that don't, and even the same societies that have had the death penalty at some point and then given it up or that have gone from not having the death penalty to including it in the administration of justice.

P: I would like to see those studies and look more closely into how they were conducted. Social phenomena are extraordinarily complex, and there can be many kinds of factors that could affect the outcome of that kind of inquiry. What else was going on in these societies at the time? What other historical events were taking place, what precedents affected the attitudes of persons? What was the overall cultural climate like, what about entertainment and the arts? What were the current religious trends and other types of social expectations? I would be extremely suspicious of those kinds of statistics without more careful analysis of their meaning and the way in which the information was gathered and interpreted. The social sciences are never as exact as the natural sciences like physics, chemistry, and biology, and there are no controlled experiments to limit the kinds of factors that might determine whether having a death penalty in place has made any difference in the numbers of violent crimes in a given society.

C: All I'm saying is that the experts report that just looking at the numbers of murders committed when a death penalty is in place as opposed to when it is not does not indicate that the death penalty provides any kind of significant deterrent to murder and that there may even be more murders when capital punishment is practiced than when it is outlawed.

P: For example, there might be deeper social forces at work that promote the commission of capital crimes and that a society responds by instituting or enforcing a death penalty so that statistically the two factors always seem to increase together.

C: Yet the statistics indicate that even within societies that go from having no capital punishment to implementing the penalty, there is actually an increase in the most serious categories of crimes.

P: Again, there could be a common cause. A society doesn't suddenly introduce a death penalty for no reason if it hasn't found the need for one before. That fact points to there being something else going on in the social order that bare statistics don't help to explain.

C: All I'm saying is that we don't make capital crimes go away by enforcing capital punishment. That kind of judicial remedy, looking at the raw evidence, only seems to make the problem worse.

P: It seems incredible to me. What's the explanation?

C: I'm not sure. But even if it's not known why such demographics obtain, the point is that there doesn't seem to be any hard scientific evidence to suggest that a society can bring about a decrease in its murder rate by instituting capital punishment and executing its worst criminals. It just doesn't seem to make any difference or have any measurable effect on patterns of serious crimes.

P: Even if that's all true, and, again, I would want to scrutinize the data and the methodology by which it is collected and interpreted in a very careful way, there's one sense in which the death penalty constitutes a definite and unmistakable deterrent to serious crime. When someone who has been found guilty of a capital crime and exhausted all appeals is finally put to death, at least we can be sure that that person is not going to commit any more crimes. That sort of deterrent cannot be denied. We should recognize that the use of the death penalty has almost always been reserved for repeat offenders who have committed multiple crimes or already been imprisoned for serious offenses.

C: We can achieve the same effect by sentencing those kinds of hard-core criminals to life imprisonment without the possibility of parole.

P: That's also idealistic rather than realistic. Hardened criminals sometimes escape from prison, and when they do, they are so desperate not to be apprehended and returned to prison, or they are so powerfully motivated to continue their violence against society, that they very frequently commit additional crimes of the same type for which they were originally imprisoned. That can't happen, needless to say, if they are executed; for in that case they are removed altogether from any possibility of further wrongdoing. The death penalty entails final justice and the absolute guarantee that the condemned will not commit more crimes.

C: That's true, although I think you might be exaggerating the possibility of dangerous criminals escaping from prison and causing further harm.

P: On the contrary, it happens all the time. Don't you watch the news?

C: Well, maybe. Anyway, some social scientists and moral philosophers argue that capital punishment doesn't deter others from committing capital crimes because it has the effect of cheapening the sense of value of human life in the community, of setting a bad example in the government's own practice of what some critics call legalized murder on the part of the state. The psychological impact of this kind of thing is probably hard to measure, but it has been conjectured that by allowing the death penalty as a punishment, the justice system actually encourages more crimes of the same sort by announcing to the world that society considers it morally acceptable to end someone's life as a response to something they have done. If that is the message subliminally received by persons in a social setting, then it should not be too surprising that persons whose behavior is shaped in large part by the norms and standards that are established by the highest authorities in the social order should also find it morally permissible in their own lives and in their own interactions with other persons, if sufficiently provoked, to resort to acts of murderous violence. Why not, if the society as a whole sanctions and condones such actions?

P: Wait a minute. The idea is that the practice of capital punishment inures citizens to the taking of life, erodes an attitude about the sanctity of human life, and sets a bad example for everyone? I'm not sure I believe that. I'd like to know what kind of scientific statistical evidence there could be for that kind of conclusion. It sounds like pure conjecture to me. Why wouldn't capital punishment have just the opposite effect, of making a convincing demonstration of society's absolute intolerance of murder and other capital offenses, to such an extent that the perpetrators of such actions are punished in the most extreme way possible? Doesn't it send the opposite message as the one you're concerned about if a society merely warehouses its worst criminals in prison for life, allows them to live out their natural lives, when they have killed other persons? What does society say about the value of the lives of the *victims* of such crimes when it allows the criminals to continue to live, even if they must do so in prison? I can imagine some persons interpreting the failure to execute criminals for capital crimes as sending the signal that the act of murdering a person is not serious enough for the murderer to pay for the crime in the only appropriate comparable way by being required to forfeit his or her own life.

C: I don't see that.

P: If murder is the worst thing you can do to another person, taking away the indispensable prerequisite for all other value a person might have in this life, then why shouldn't society demonstrate the seriousness with which it views such an act by depriving the guilty perpetrators of such an offense in the most extreme possible way? The worst crimes deserve the worst penalties, if there is to be justice at all. In the case of a crime like cold-blooded premeditated murder, a just society owes its members the dignity of refusing those who have taken away other persons' lives the continuance of their own lives. How can we morally justify permitting a murderer to experience life even with whatever limited enjoyments might be found in prison when their victims have had their lives irrevocably taken away from them? And please don't hit me with the same tired old slogan we agreed to bracket before, that two wrongs don't make a right.

C: But what if we're wrong in sentencing someone to death? What if we send the wrong person to the lethal injection chamber, and the condemned was innocent all along?

P: I thought we've been over this ground already.

C: In a way, we have. But if mistakes are possible, as we know they are, then we can after all justify allowing those who are convicted of committing even the most horrible crimes to live, at least for the rest of their natural lives in prison without possibility of parole, on the off chance that an error might have been made in judicial proceedings in finding them guilty.

There have been several cases lately of persons who had been wrongly sentenced and were later found innocent as a result of improved scientific techniques, such as DNA testing. Who knows what further advances might eventually be discovered to reevaluate other verdicts? And this is to say nothing about judicial decisions falsely reached because of emotional reactions to current public events on the part of judges or juries; political aspects of certain trials; prejudices, including racial and other kinds of biases; a lynch mob mentality that can affect some legal proceedings; and the like.

A good case is the mistaken sentencing of the German immigrant, Bruno Hauptmann, found guilty of kidnapping and murdering the infant son of Charles Lindbergh. The evidence was circumstantial, and there was a great desire to find someone guilty for this terrible crime. The accused was a foreign naturalized citizen from a country with which the United States had been at war, and there was a heated sentiment that the man must have been guilty. Prejudice may have clouded the sort of careful judgment that is really needed by a judge and jury members. The man was found guilty in the so-called Crime of the Century and executed in the electric chair. Most authorities today regard the sentencing as wrong and the execution as unjustified. If a mistake was made, there was no way to correct it or give the man his life back. The only possibility of redressing that kind of wrongful sentencing is if the accused and convicted are not executed.

P: I've already agreed that the prosecution of capital punishment is a serious affair and that mistakes, if they occur, are profoundly regrettable.

C: But you don't regard the problem as warranting the elimination of capital punishment.

P: No, as I've said, because of what I take to be the positive benefits of recognizing the importance of life and the extreme evil of committing capital crimes, to protect society from the worst criminals and to serve the requirements of justice.

C: Anyway, regardless of what we think, say, or do, the Supreme Court can outlaw capital punishment at any point. Look at the paper. It says right here that the highest court in the land is considering the constitutionality of execution by lethal injection as potentially cruel and unusual punishment. If they rule against this form of the death penalty, then it doesn't matter what we decide over coffee and tea, all bets will be off. We might as well stop wasting our time debating all this stuff in a vacuum.

P: I couldn't disagree with you more. Whether or not the Supreme Court approves or decides to shoot down the death penalty generally or by any specific method, what we're talking about is still absolutely relevant to the ethics of capital punishment. We're not questioning the *legality* but the *morality* of capital punishment. The law isn't always right. If the court upholds capital punishment or makes it illegal, we still need to worry about whether it was morally right to do so. And we still need to ask whether other countries that aren't subject to our laws or our example are or are not right to institute or prohibit capital punishment. It never follows from the mere fact that something is or is not the case that therefore it ought or ought not to be the case.

C: I agree. If we're looking at these problems ethically, philosophically, then we can't so easily get ourselves off the hook by relegating all moral authority in this or any other matter to the legislature or judiciary at any level within the government.

P: Then I guess if you're willing we'd better pick this up again where we had to end things today. We haven't really resolved anything, but I think I'm starting to get a better sense of why you're so opposed to capital punishment.

2

❦

Day Two: Justice and the Morality of Compassion

L ate afternoon at the student union. A large flat-screen television over-head is broadcasting a national twenty-four-hour news bulletin program. Students are passing through with books and backpacks, sipping soft drinks and bottled water, chatting and laughing. C has already been waiting fifteen minutes for P. Plugged into an mp3 player, C pops out one earphone as P approaches.

C: You're late.

P: French exam.

C: How'd you do?

P: Won't hear until next week. What about our discussion of capital punishment? Are you ready to take this on again?

C: Absolutely. And here's what I propose. Let's do a quick recap of where we wound up yesterday. I'll give you my impression of the arguments each of us made and how they stood up against criticisms. You can refine my summary if you want and fill in any gaps, and afterward we can begin to look in more detail into the positions we've been defending. That will set the stage for some new topics and additional arguments also, including some of the problems we touched on previously but decided to postpone until later. What do you think?

P: Good idea.

C: I'll get us rolling. You support the death penalty for certain kinds of crimes under certain kinds of conditions, and I'm completely opposed.

P: On that we are most definitely agreed.

C: I wanted to argue that capital punishment was uncivilized, by which I didn't mean that civilizations in the true sense of the word have not implemented a death penalty. I had in mind something more like a normative rather than historical or anthropologically descriptive sense of the word "civilized." To me, to be civilized means that a society upholds the highest standards of moral conduct. You managed to convince me, though, that if by "civilized" we just mean living in a city, which is the literal meaning of the word, or exemplifying other aspects of high culture in the arts and sciences and social institutions, then historically as well as today there are many civilizations that have practiced the death penalty.

P: If that's right, and if what you mean by "civilized" is just whatever moral standards you accept, then we can make some progress by forgetting about the civilized or uncivilized nature of capital punishment and just focus on whatever standards of morality you think are correct. Maybe I'll agree with them, maybe not. Then we can try to see what implications your standards actually have with respect to the death penalty question.

C: I'm with that. Fine.

P: The problem now is that you're going to be committed in the normative sense of the word "civilized" to saying that many civilizations are uncivilized.

C: Actually, that's a conclusion I want to avoid. I'm doing so by simply granting you the word "civilized" in the historical-anthropological sense and giving up altogether my use of the word in the normative or ethically loaded sense. From now on, I'm not going to raise the issue of whether capital punishment is civilized. You've convinced me. Instead, I'm going to argue that capital punishment is just plain morally wrong.

P: That's progress. Of course, I'm going to continue to argue that capital punishment, properly administered, for certain kinds of crimes, is not only morally permissible but actually morally obligatory and in that regard morally right. Ideally, I will say, we wouldn't need capital punishment because no one in a moral utopia would ever commit such horrendous actions. It's their antisocial behavior that has obliged freedom-loving societies to institute the death penalty in accord with the requirements of justice. They've come to the conclusion that it's the only way to maintain order for the sake of persons who want to live in peace and harmony.

C: Peace and harmony, huh? Well, our differences are coming into sharper perspective all the time.

P: What I recall of the main arguments we talked about is that I was maintaining that the death penalty is not only morally appropriate but strictly demanded by the requirements of justice in the case of murder, extreme violence, treason, and possibly other categories of crimes, whereas you held that the death penalty was cruel and unusual punishment, uncivilized in that sense, even if you don't want to use that word any more. You were saying that in any event the death penalty can't be morally justified as providing a deterrent to heinous crimes because sociological studies show scientifically that crimes of violence are actually statistically positively correlated with the institution and application of the death penalty. There's an increase in homicide when the death penalty is applied and a decrease whenever the death penalty is abolished or when there's a moratorium on its implementation. Is that it?

C: Well, not quite. I was also arguing that the death penalty is morally wrong and ought to be unlawful because it constitutes a kind of punishment that cannot be undone. There is no correction or restitution for persons who have been wrongly put to death for crimes, and recent studies prove that many persons have been wrongfully sentenced to death. In some cases, those death sentences have actually been carried out, while in others persons have been released after years of being mistakenly imprisoned.

Some of those prisoners have been awaiting execution and have thankfully been reprieved through the emergence of new facts, including DNA evidence, that were unavailable when they were originally sentenced to death. My point is that we allow no margin for error when we carry out a death sentence because we cannot resurrect executed prisoners when it turns out later that they were wrongfully convicted. If those prisoners had simply been sentenced to life in prison without the possibility of parole, then we would have served all the requirements of justice, and we would have allowed ourselves a margin of error whereby if a mistaken judgment of guilt is handed down by a judge or jury, we can still do something later to try to rectify the error.

Once a death sentence is carried out, we cannot undo the wrong that may have occurred. I would say accordingly that justice and the presumption of innocence until actually proven guilty requires that we do not impose a death penalty even for persons convicted of the worst kinds of crimes. We should never have the arrogance to suppose that the judicial system cannot make mistakes, and, wherever possible, where human lives are concerned, we should always do our best to make sure that we can undo a mistaken judgment. We cannot meet this fundamental requirement of justice if we execute criminals, but we can do so by substituting the more humane sentence of life in prison without the possibility of parole. On top of that, I deny, on the grounds of scientific comparisons that have been conducted concerning correlations of murder and other crimes of violence with the institution and implementation of the death penalty, that a society's practice of capital punishment serves as any kind of deterrent to serious crimes.

P: All of this requires more investigation and argument.

C: Granted.

P: Now let's also take stock of whatever more basic points of agreement exist between us.

C: I suppose that if we didn't agree about many things, then we couldn't argue and disagree about other matters in the first place.

P: True. I think so too.

C: So, what do you have in mind?

P: Well, I was struck yesterday by the fact that we are both appalled by the kinds of crimes that societies have tried to address by instituting a death penalty. It's not as though I think that murdering someone is an act deserving the most severe possible punishment under the law and you think that murder is okay. Right? I mean, you don't have the attitude that persons who are otherwise in their right minds should be free to simply continue doing what they do as though nothing had happened after they kill or torture their victims. I think and I hope we agree that wrongdoing of this magnitude deserves some sort of serious meaningful legal response.

C: Absolutely.

P: And I think I'm also right to suppose that we don't want innocent persons who might be falsely accused of crimes to suffer needlessly or to have unjust or inhumane sentences imposed on them.

C: Right again. This is without question common ground between us, whatever other differences of opinion we might have about exactly how to implement these goals and how we should try to realize our moral ideals.

P: Good. This is helpful.

C: We would both like to see crime diminished and violent criminals punished. What divides us is the question of what the most morally correct and legally effective punishment might be.

P: That's correct. And neither of us, I think it's also fair to say, wants to be excessively lenient or excessively harsh in the treatment of criminals. We both want to have the rule of law properly instituted and enforced within a framework of a correct morality, whatever that turns out to be. We're not deluded about the kinds of crimes some people commit, and, equally, I hope, we're also not unrealistic about the possibility of false accusation, prosecution, conviction, or sentencing or, for that matter, about what can and cannot happen to persons once they're serving a sentence behind bars. We both recognize that rehabilitation is never guaranteed and that prisoners sometimes escape from prison and cause havoc if the authorities are not sufficiently vigilant.

C: Exactly.

P: Above all else, I think it's true to say also that we are both open-minded about whether capital punishment is ultimately morally justified. I mean by this that while you now have what you consider to be good reasons to oppose the death penalty, and I have what I consider to be good reasons for supporting the death penalty in at least some extreme cases, we are not trying to be dogmatic or inflexible in our opinions. If you posed a truly convincing argument against capital punishment, then I would follow you in your objections. I would simply change my mind on the basis of a good solid line of reasoning and come over to your side by agreeing that there is no adequate justification for an enlightened progressive society to execute persons for any crime, no matter how severe or treacherous. I don't expect that to happen because I think my reasons are stronger, but I'm willing to be persuaded.

C: Absolutely. And I for my part in the meantime am also willing to change my position if you were to persuade me that the death penalty is sometimes warranted.

P: We're together on that too. If we didn't share this attitude, then I suppose there'd be no real point in discussing the issue. I imagine that if either of us thought we knew beyond the possibility of a shadow of a doubt that we were right, we might still try to help each other to see the light. But the fact is, we're now convinced but not inflexible in our convictions that we each have the right answers and that these answers are logically opposed.

C: All true. With that foundation to work with, I think we can now proceed to sharpen our differences and see if we can't work our way toward some more satisfying answer. The differences we have are just reflections of differences of moral and political opinion in society at large. My view represents one major division within this social debate, and yours represents the other, opposite, point of view.

P: At first it seems that you didn't consider the death penalty to be a punishment in the proper sense of the word at all. Did I finally convince you that it is? Have you had any further thoughts about whether execution constitutes a punishment?

C: It's certainly not a punishment in the sense of a penalty someone is made to pay in order to correct his or her future behavior.

P: Not the execution itself, of course, but how about the death sentence?

C: Do you mean the fact that the condemned person must live at least for a time with the knowledge that he or she is going to be executed for having committed a crime?

P: Yes.

C: We can call that the Dostoyevsky factor, from our discussion yesterday. As you already know, I consider that to be part of what makes the death penalty cruel and unusual punishment.

P: Vague words. In some sense, any punishment is cruel and unusual. If a practice isn't cruel in the only relevant sense of causing pain or discomfort of some sort or other, then it's not punishment. Any punishment is also bound to be unusual in the sense that being punished at all is by definition something unusual. As I said yesterday, I think the Constitution's phrase is used either because the authors of the document were squeamish about using the word "torture" or because they thought the term was too vague to have a proper role in the statement of law. What is torture, after all?

C: I would say it's causing pain and suffering.

P: Not good enough. Remember the dentist and doctor. They sometimes cause unavoidable pain and suffering in the interests of health, but, except in a very loose sense of the word, that doesn't constitute either torture or punishment.

C: Okay. So, let me try again. Torture is causing pain and suffering without consideration of trying to improve the victim's bodily welfare.

P: That's better, I guess. But it still doesn't completely sew things up. After all, in a war a soldier causes pain and suffering without consideration of the victim's bodily welfare, but we wouldn't ordinarily say that all of the mayhem that soldiers are required to create necessarily constitutes torture. War is a terrible thing, of course, greatly to be avoided and regretted, but, still, killing and injury in war is one thing, and torture is something else. Sometimes soldiers also commit acts of torture, but it's not as though any violence that a soldier commits during war automatically qualifies as torture, though under your new definition it would.

C: Fair enough. But there is such a thing as torture, and soldiers and other persons who are guilty of it are sometimes judged according to standards of wrongful behavior, so it must be possible in principle to say what torture is. Torture is prohibited by the Geneva Convention and by other treaties and legal precedents governing conduct during war and in everyday life. When a case of torture comes before a court-martial or civilian judge and jury, the law must have some idea of what it's talking about.

P: I wouldn't put too much faith philosophically in what the law does. As a practical matter, lots of concepts are treated in a very careless and imprecise way by the courts.

C: I'm starting to see that the concept of cruel behavior is a rather slippery concept, hard to define. Let me try this: torture is causing pain and suffering without trying to improve the victim's bodily welfare when the victim is not physically able to flee or retaliate.

P: That's interesting. I wonder if that covers all the cases. What we want out of a good definition is not only that the concept to be defined and the concept whereby it is defined refer to precisely the same thing but also that the definition tells us something new, something we did not already have to understand about the concept being defined in order to understand its definition. I think you're definitely getting closer.

C: Right. A definition always has two parts: a *definiendum* as the concept to be defined and the *definiens* as the concept or concepts that define the concept of the *definiendum*. In a good definition, the *definiendum* and *definiens* are informatively codesignative. They designate the exact same thing, and they do so in a way that tells us something we did not already know.

P: Then, if your most recent definition of torture, of cruel and unusual punishment as a euphemism for torture, is causing pain and suffering without trying to improve the victim's bodily welfare when the victim is not physically able to flee or retaliate, what about the soldier who kills an enemy combatant who is unable to escape? Suppose you have an enemy soldier who has been cornered and has no chance of fleeing, and you as a soldier fighting for your country, out of ammunition, kill the soldier in what turns out to be a painful way that causes the trapped soldier to experience quite a bit of pain. Suppose you have to strangle or use a crude weapon that does not bring about a quick and easy death but causes lots of suffering. That might not be the most courageous act on the part of a soldier, although military strategy might require it and the rules of engagement in war might permit it, but it certainly doesn't seem like torture.

C: I think you're right. There's something more deliberate and unnecessary about an act of torture. It's done, unlike the dentist and physician and even the soldier in the field, simply for the sake of causing pain.

P: And yet, advocates of using torture in military situations and information gathering sometimes argue that causing pain is necessary in order to obtain information needed to help save the lives of others. Now, if that's your latest version of the definition, then notice that you can no longer object to capital punishment as torture or cruel and unusual punishment. I don't think even the most ardent opponent of the death penalty would say that executing a criminal is done simply or solely for the sake of causing pain. In fact, neither the death sentence, contrary to the Dostoyevsky factor, nor carrying out the death sentence, are necessarily intended to cause pain, and neither needs actually cause any pain. Some psychological types will experience a certain amount of trauma knowing that they are to be executed, while others may be so hardened that they will not. We've already said that in principle there can be methods of execution that are completely painless. If that were not true, then there could be no possible grounds for considering an act of euthanasia as morally permissible. Think of the execution of a convicted criminal who has exhausted all possible appeals and for whom no scientific evidence holds out the prospect of overturning the conviction, after due process and a careful consideration of all the relevant facts, as an act of euthanasia. The criminal is simply put to sleep.

C: Do you mean the way we put a dog to sleep when it's gotten too old or too sick, when it exhibits unacceptable habits like biting people, or when there's just no one who wants to give it a home?

P: There's an analogy, perhaps, but I'm not trying to say that even the worst criminals don't deserve to be treated better than dogs.

C: I hope not.

P: No, of course. Look, by that reasoning we would be acting morally objectionably even by putting criminals in jail since we do that also to dogs when they're impounded. You can't object to that in principle, right? Because, after all, you are saying that the worst criminals should be incarcerated for life, in some instances, without possibility of parole, rather than being executed. And being locked up behind bars is something we also sometimes do to dogs.

C: Agreed. There are always analogies, but they don't always prove that what is similar is exactly the same.

P: That's a relief. So, why not recognize that certain kinds of criminal behavior invoke principles of justice that can be satisfied only by painlessly executing a perpetrator? We don't want to cause the individual excessive pain, and perhaps execution by hanging, electrocution, asphyxiation by cyanide gas, and beheading, among other methods, are unnecessarily painful. But what is morally objectionable about serving the demands of justice by painless execution?

C: Several things, I think. Let me start with this . . .

P: Do you grant at least in the case of a painless method of execution, let us say, lethal injection, that if the procedure proves to be quick and entirely painless, then it does not constitute torture or inherently cruel and unusual punishment?

C: "Inherently" is the operative word here. Just because the method often or even usually works properly and the executed person doesn't typically experience any trauma or pain doesn't mean that there isn't always the potential for things to go wrong.

P: But nothing is perfect in the world of practical affairs.

C: I know. But if we are administering justice, then it is unforgivable to risk a condemned person's suffering a botched execution. We don't have to execute anyone at all, remember. We can keep them in jail for life.

P: And you don't think that's cruel and unusual? You don't think it's a torture to condemn someone to live out his or her days in a tiny cell with crappy food and no opportunity to live a normal life? To spend all one's time in the company of individuals who may even be more dangerous than oneself? Do you know how many inmates in the prison system are killed, injured, raped, and generally terrified by the company they have to keep?

C: It's bad, I know. But if they are convicted and they have exhausted their appeals, then this is what they deserve.

P: But they don't deserve a quick and painless death?

C: No. I still don't think so.

P: Well, why on earth not?

C: Because, when we execute a criminal, we're playing God.

P: Ah, there it is. I knew we'd reach this point sooner or later. What do you mean by "playing God"?

C: Taking the life of someone is playing God. Only God can decide who lives and who dies.

P: But you don't even believe in God. You told me last semester that you're an agnostic most of the time and an outright atheist when you're being completely honest with yourself.

C: What I mean by "playing God" is just a phrase. You don't have to believe in the existence of God in order to object to an individual or a government doing what's called "playing God."

P: See, I think that if you don't believe in the existence of God, then you should try to put your objection in different words. If you have no better way to express your objection to certain kinds of public policy decisions than to refer to something you don't even believe in yourself, then you are either trying to make some kind of irrational emotional appeal in support of a belief or you have simply not thought through your own position carefully enough to be able to articulate your exact reasons for objecting to capital punishment. Perhaps your real underlying grounds for objecting to the death penalty are just emotional after all, and you don't have any good arguments against it. Talking about "playing God" just disguises whatever it is that might be a sound basis for accepting or rejecting a position that you then try to pretend is somehow more deeply ethical. I'm not buying it.

C: Well, I can tell you what I mean by "playing God," and when I have, then maybe you won't think it's all just touchy-feely but has a more solid basis.

P: Go right ahead and be my guest.

C: "Playing God" means making a life-or-death decision for someone that you don't absolutely need to make for the good of anyone's welfare. Thus, I wouldn't say that a doctor deciding to save one patient rather than another when there is only enough medicine for one individual is playing God. The physician is just doing his or her duty, acting responsibly as a health care professional. The doctor is in fact deciding who should live and who should die, but that's still not what I would call playing God because under the unfortunate circumstances, there's no free choice. If you're playing God, then it's like the gods that Homer portrays in his great epic poem the *Iliad*, where the divinities decide to support one side of a battle rather than the other often for entirely vain or trivial reasons, sometimes just because it suits their desires or flatters their vanity to have that kind of role in the lives of human beings. The point is that if there's no absolute necessity to causing another human being to die, then we are playing God in the sense of the Homeric gods—in whose existence, by the way, I also don't believe. We are acting as though we were entitled to have the power of life and death over our fellow human beings when there is no compelling rational justification for us to be making such a decision one way or the other.

C: I'm really not sure about the whole atheist–agnostic thing. Sometimes I think I am an agnostic after all rather than an atheist. That is, I don't claim to know with certainty there is no God, and I am deeply impressed by some of the religious teachings against violence that one finds in the New Testament about loving others. I know there are many hypocritical, so-called Christians, but I find inspiring people like Martin Luther King Jr., who in the name of love and compassion sought to confront powerful racial barriers in our country. And I regard Mahatma Gandhi also as deeply impressive. While I do not belong to any specific denomination, I have attended Quaker services and admire their history of standing up for nonviolence. Anyway, I'm open to arguments from the standpoint of religious conviction about the immorality of capital punishment.

P: Fair enough. But in our argument about the death penalty, we can't very well bring in religious reasons for or against capital punishment. First of all, to do so would be in violation of the separation of church and state. Second, you can find lots of religions and traditions within a religion like Christianity (for King) and Hinduism (for Gandhi) that support capital punishment.

C: I am not proposing the imposition of a religion on society. I am instead highlighting what might be called a strong spiritual case for opposing capital punishment based on extensive teachings across many religions on the centrality of loving enemies and showing mercy. Look, I might come to the point where I agree with you that capital punishment can be deserved. Maybe, if you maliciously killed an innocent person, you would have no right to complain if society executed you. But does society have to do this, morally speaking? Wouldn't it be more merciful to spare a criminal's life, especially if the person confesses and is deeply remorseful and repentent?

P: This all still seems a little too "spiritual" in my book. Talk of repentance seems largely a religious notion.

C: It is featured in some religions, but it's not exclusively faith based. I also don't understand what seems to be your hostility to bringing in what I am calling "spiritual reasons."

P: Define "spiritual."

C: I'm not sure I could do that clearly, but I suspect that with the Quakers, in nonviolent movements in Christianity, Hinduism, Buddhism, Taoism, and other religious traditions, there is an appeal to the enormous importance of human beings, even for those who fail morally. In some of these traditions, persons may be considered made in the image of God. These traditions thereby affirm the vast importance of not giving up on other human beings when they have sinned against others, even when they've committed murder.

P: You're being rather selective in appealing to religious teachings, aren't you? Many religions denounce homosexuality, for example. Would you say also that we should therefore prohibit homosexuality, make it illegal, and punish it as a crime?

C: Not in my view. Yes, I suppose I am being selective in identifying particular religious or spiritual reasons that I find deeply moving and revelatory of genuine moral values. But I think that you are also being selective in terms of those parts of the theory of justice to which you want to appeal.

P: What kind of spiritual values do you have in mind?

C: Consider what Avery Cardinal Dulles says in his 2001 article "Catholicism and Capital Punishment." It was published as a contribution to *First Things: The Journal of Religion, Culture, and Public Life*. I brought a copy along just for our discussion today. Cardinal Dulles explains that in the Old Testament, there were many kinds of offenses that were punished by the death penalty. He points out that the law of Moses speaks of thirty-six capital offenses for which execution by stoning, burning, decapitation, or strangulation is prescribed. The list of death penalty transgressions includes idolatry, magic, blasphemy, violation of the Sabbath, murder, adultery, bestiality, pederasty, and incest.

P: There, you see what I'm talking about?

C: Well, wait. . . . The cardinal also points out that the New Testament doesn't explicitly forbid capital punishment either. And the Catholic Church itself has supported the death penalty through much of its history.

P: Okay. Then what's the objection, and how did a conservative religious body reverse itself on this question when it's got so much tradition standing behind it?

C: Dulles doesn't see this as a reversal but perhaps as something more like a clarification.

P: Oh, I see . . .

C: Now, don't be cynical. The idea is that only God is supposed to have ultimate jurisdiction over matters of life and death. The modern Church understands its rising objections to capital punishment as consistent with its ban on abortion and euthanasia as a violation of every human being's right to life. The cardinal also identifies four purposes of punishment for which there has been long-standing univocal support by Church authorities. These include rehabilitation, defense against the criminal, deterrence, and just retribution. He argues that the death penalty is not consistent with all these objectives but that enlightened incarceration of those capital criminals that would otherwise have been sentenced to death is the only proper way to satisfy all four of these goals for the administration of secular criminal justice.

P: So, you're saying that we're playing God or acting like the gods when we sentence someone to death or carry out a death sentence execution because we don't actually need to?

C: That's right. Nothing compels us to execute a criminal. We can simply keep them in prison for the rest of their natural lives.

P: You're certainly right that the situation in the judicial system is different than the situation facing a doctor who can only save one of two patients with limited medicine. If the doctor has to decide who will live and who will die, then the decision might be made on a number of different morally defensible grounds. There is still most definitely an element of circumstantial compulsion, unless the doctor simply shrugs his or her shoulders and decides to let both patients die for lack of a good reason to save patient 1 rather than patient 2.

C: Exactly. That's what I mean. Nothing forces us to execute a criminal. If we—and I mean society, the law—chooses to do so, it's because we have taken on ourselves a godlike role, deciding without any real compulsion who is to live and who is to die. I find that morally objectionable.

P: Why?

C: Why? What do you mean, why?

P: I mean, what do you find morally objectionable about doing what justice requires in the case of persons who commit horrible crimes?

C: Why should someone have to die who would otherwise not need to die?

P: Well, in the case of the kinds of criminals we're talking about, because they themselves have played God, deciding on the basis usually of their own selfish motives or sometimes through sheer stupidity that an innocent person who happens to fall under their power should die. What better, indeed, what other appropriate punishment can there possibly be for such a person than to forfeit his or her own life?

C: But we should never be in a position to make that kind of decision.

P: Maybe not. But I ask you again, *why*, exactly, not? Let me remind you of the kind of criminals we're talking about. Do you remember hearing on the news about a relatively recent murder in Florida? The victim was a nine-year-old girl, Jessica Marie Lundsford, who was raped, beaten, and then buried alive in a shallow grave in two black plastic garbage bags about 400 feet away from her own home. She had been abducted, held captive for several days, and sexually abused. She was found buried alive clutching a stuffed animal that she must have loved.

C: Who did it?

P: A forty-six-year-old convicted sex offender, named John Evander Couey, confessed and was convicted of the crime. Where is God or the gods when that kind of thing happens? Who is supposed to do what we expect of real meaningful justice when that kind of crime is committed?

C: I'm not saying that the monster who committed that crime shouldn't be punished. I'm saying that killing the killer won't bring the dead girl back and that we cheapen our own sense of right and wrong when we kill, even if we do it as painlessly as possible with lethal injection or whatever other method is devised. In a sense, we punish the criminals more severely by making them spend their lives thinking about what they did than if we simply put them to death. I'm not so sure that lethal injection is all that painless, by the way. I've heard some very disturbing things on the news.

P: That's a rather naive point of view, if you don't mind my saying so.

C: How so?

P: Well, many of these criminals don't care at all how badly or how wrongly they've acted from our point of view. Some of them actually enjoy reliving the events of their crimes. They're not repentant, even if they say they are when they come up before a parole board or when they're trying to wheedle special privileges out of the authorities.

C: You're too cynical.

P: Am I? Well, how do you think you'd feel if that little nine-year-old girl who was raped, beaten, and buried alive with her stuffed toy was your sister or your own daughter?

C: I don't know how I'd feel. I can't say. It's too awful, of course. I can't really imagine it, having everything taken away like that by some stupid person's selfish desire. Maybe I'd want revenge.

P: Some people do, and some don't.

C: The question is, What's the appropriate response? And should the wish for revenge play any part in the prosecution of justice?

P: The law is there to serve the needs of those who obey it.

C: I suppose that's true. But I don't think we should give in to our emotions, no matter how strongly we feel about something, where another person's life is concerned. If we do, then we make ourselves just as bad as the criminals.

P: How can you say that? I don't understand that kind of thinking at all. We're not as bad as the criminals when we want them to pay an appropriate price for what they've done. That little girl was innocent, like all the victims of these senseless violent crimes. The criminal who takes a life isn't on a par with someone who has been victimized. The criminal chooses to kill or rape or hurt another person. We as a society have the opportunity through the just application of the law to make it clear that we do not accept and will not tolerate that kind of crime, that the lives and happiness of the persons who are affected by violence matter to us, that they are more important than those who try to place themselves above the law by ignoring the most basic rules of decent human conduct.

C: I think that what you're describing does just the opposite by showing that we don't care enough about people's lives to refrain from executing criminals.

P: *Innocent* lives is what we need to care about. That and the suffering caused to the families and survivors of those who are brutally killed in the commission of a crime.

C: All life is sacred.

P: I don't think you really believe that.

C: Of course I do.

P: Well, then, you should be a total vegetarian.

C: I am.

P: And you should refuse to wear leather; no leather belts or shoes or other objects.

C: I don't do that.

P: And that's not all. You don't really believe that all life is sacred because if you are a vegetarian, you are at least eating vegetables, and before they're harvested, vegetables are also alive. If all life is sacred, then you should refuse to eat vegetables too. If you did that, of course, in all consistency, then you wouldn't be respecting your own life because you have to eat something in order to stay alive. To live and to sustain life is to eat something that was once alive. That's the way of the world. It all depends on where you find yourself in the great food chain.

C: Nonhuman animals are in a special category, different from plants. Most animals, unlike vegetables, have feelings, a kind of conscious life. That's why I don't want to eat animal food.

P: Very good. But it means that you don't really regard *all* life as sacred in the sense that you don't want to have any moral responsibility for the death or use of any and all living things that requires their death.

C: Okay, okay. You're right. What I really wanted to say is that I believe all *human* life, innocent or guilty of any crime, is sacred.

P: I'll bet you don't really believe that, either. What about abortion in the earliest stages? Do you support a woman's right to abortion in the first trimester of a pregnancy? What about euthanasia, in which a person suffering horribly from an incurable disease is painlessly put to death at his or her own request?

C: Believe it or not, I'm completely undecided about the morality of abortion when a fetus is healthy and not threatening the life of the mother. I know it's a popular view to think that abortion is part of a woman's rights to reproductive self-determination, but I'm not absolutely sure that abortion is morally permissible. I just don't know. I think that the issue is very complicated, and I think that there are strong arguments both for and against the ethics of abortion.

P: How about war? Are you totally and absolutely against war in any and every circumstance? Do you think there's simply no such thing as a just war in which it becomes necessary to kill human beings in order to secure freedom or prevent injustices on a vast scale by rogue governments like the Nazis in the 1940s?

C: Always the Nazis.

P: I know. It's a rather overworked example. But they're a convenient illustration of a pretty clear-cut case of evil unleashed on the world that most people would say called for extreme action in a justified war. If some people hadn't united and fought against the Third Reich, just imagine what they would have done. As it is, they exterminated many millions of innocent people. How else can you stop that kind of thing from happening unless you are willing to take lives in the course of conducting military operations against the forces of evil? And if that's right, what happens to your idea that all human life is sacred? You can't retreat now and say you just meant all *innocent* human life is sacred because that's a position with which I also, with appropriate qualifications, can agree. Remember that, where the death penalty for capital crimes is concerned, we're not talking about innocent persons but persons guilty of some of the most terrible crimes.

C: I know. I don't like war, either.

P: Right. Well, who does? It would be a better world if there were no wars and no need for any wars, including wars that we try to convince ourselves are morally justified. But it's not a perfect world, and we have to consider our moral responsibilities in the actual world with all its flaws and disappointments just as we find it. Anything else would be morally irresponsible and a dereliction of our duty to fulfill our obligations toward those who need our help when injustice threatens.

C: You're not going to ask me whether I would have assassinated Adolf Hitler prior to 1939 if I'd had the chance, are you?

P: I wasn't going to. But since you've brought it up, would you?

C: I couldn't do it personally, I don't think. But knowing what we know now, I guess I wouldn't have objected if someone else had done it.

P: Then once again you're just shirking your personal responsibility. It's always easier to let someone else do the dirty work that morality sometimes requires. Did I just say that? Anyway, in the case of capital punishment, no one would be asking you to become a professional executioner for the state. We're talking only about whether the death penalty should be practiced, not who should do it on a personal level or how they should do it, either, for that matter, as long as it's physically humane.

C: I still want to say that in some sense all human life, innocent or guilty, is sacred, and that we're playing God if we take it on ourselves to decide who lives and who dies when there's no absolute necessity to do so.

P: Even that formulation isn't exactly right yet. I don't want to sound too nitpicking, but consider a cancerous tumor growing in a human body. It's alive and it's human—just count the number of chromosomes in its cells, and you'll see that it's a living human thing. But you wouldn't hesitate at all if you had cancer to have the tumor surgically removed and destroyed or killed with chemicals or radiation in order to save your own life.

C: That's stretching things a little far, isn't it? I mean, I'm not talking about dependent human tissue but about a human being, an individual person or potential human person, whether a conscious thinking entity like you or me or possibly a fetus or someone who's deeply comatose.

P: So, the reformulation is to say that the life of any human being, innocent or guilty, is sacred in the sense that no other person should have the right, perhaps with certain exceptions for war or when acting in self-defense or the defense of other persons in imminent danger, to decide whether any human being is to live or die. Is that it?

C: That's getting closer to what I think I mean. Yes, thank you.

P: Just trying to help. I'm not necessarily looking to refute anything you're saying. I just want to understand it the best way I can so that I can make up my own mind as to whether you're on the right track.

C: Then I think that's at least part of what I want to say. It doesn't matter in the end if the death penalty decreases or increases violent crime. It doesn't matter whether an execution is painful for the condemned or completely painless and trauma free. What matters, I think, is that it's simply wrong for any human being or committee of human beings to decide that another human being, a person, I mean, of course, should die if that person does not want to die. Euthanasia is different when someone chooses to die. Abortion is different if, and this is the sticking point, as far as I'm concerned, a fetus at the very early stages of pregnancy is not a person or even in an obvious sense a potential person. In the case of an adult human being convicted of a capital crime, however, the principle is violated if that person does not want to die and is made to die because of legal proceedings. I am saying that morally no such decision should ever be taken because it goes against the idea that a person's unnecessary and involuntary death should never be caused by any other person's or group of persons' decision.

P: In the case of murder, of course, that's exactly what the killer does. He or she decides that the victim should involuntarily die.

C: That's true, of course. And that's one of the reasons why I find murder morally objectionable. It's ethically wrong for the murderer to decide that another person should die without that person's consent. That's why I think cold-blooded premeditated first-degree killers should suffer the most severe penalties available under the law, short of actually being put to death. For that reason, I believe that the most severe penalty available for acts of homicide should be life in prison without the possibility of parole.

P: It's coming into focus for me now. I think I'm beginning to get a better idea of what you're saying. But you still haven't said enough to make me understand why you take this position.

C: A convicted killer or a criminal in another category for which the death penalty is invoked is still a human being. On humanitarian grounds we owe it to ourselves, not to the criminals, to treat even the worst offenders in a way that reflects our sense of values about the importance of human life. I use the word "sacred" advisedly here, although I realize it has religious and other connotations that might be misleading. It's still a useful way to summarize the attitude to which I'm referring. It says that we will not stoop to doing what the criminals in our society are capable of doing because we are not criminals. We do not take human life when there is any other alternative choice. If you really want to know whether I would have assassinated Hitler before World War II and the European Holocaust if I could have done so, I think my answer is that I would not have done so as long as I thought there was another way of dealing with him. And, of course, from a practical point of view and within the fictional circumstances that your thought experiment conjures up, there are unlimitedly many other ways of prohibiting Hitler from wreaking the tragedy for which he was ultimately responsible. He could have been imprisoned, or he could have had his power curbed in a variety of ways. He could have been discredited so that he lost influence even within his own party. He could have been defeated in a power struggle within his own party or been deprived of funding. And so on and so on. It's too easy to say, wouldn't you have assassinated him? It's a lazy way to deal with the difficult problem of confronting a criminal mind. But there's always a solution, if we look hard enough for it, that doesn't require that we actually take the life of another human being.

P: I'm skeptical as to whether anything like that could have actually worked.

C: I see. But you're not skeptical about my being able to travel back in time, secure a weapon and get into Hitler's company in close enough proximity to assassinate him, and then actually commit the act?

P: The point of the thought experiment is just to test your own willingness to take drastic action against someone whom we know in retrospect will otherwise create enormous evil. It's all fictional; it's just a question of what your own moral principles permit or require you to do.

C: Well, I think I've just told you. I wouldn't kill him if there was any other remote possibility of stopping him without taking his life. We don't disagree about the fact that Hitler was one of the world's worst homicidal monsters. The question is whether the only way of preventing him from perpetrating his crimes is by taking his life. I think that with a little ingenuity in the thought experiment scenario, we can come up with a lot of different possibilities that would have the same result of changing history for the better.

P: Let's pursue this example for a while, then, if you don't mind. You're saying that what would be wrong is not interfering in any way with Hitler's life but specifically killing him. You speak of the immorality of killing someone when that person doesn't choose or doesn't want to die. But most persons are in that situation generally, unless they are contemplating suicide or have a living will or other expression of the desire to be euthanized under the most extreme circumstances. So, I think we can just discount the "involuntary" killing part and assume that, except in these unusual cases, any criminal whose life might come under jeopardy by the death penalty or in a situation like the Hitler assassination thought experiment does not want to die. Then we are only thinking about killing someone who does not voluntarily choose to die. Is that correct?

C: Right. I just want to make provision in the statement of my moral principle for the case of suicide and euthanasia that you had mentioned earlier on. Let's just agree that we're talking about taking someone's life against their will.

P: Then consider this alternative. You limit your principle in the present case at least to not actually killing a person who has committed a capital crime or, in the Hitler scenario, is known in retrospect to be on the brink of committing mass murder. So, I have to ask, Would you find it morally objectionable in such cases simply to destroy the person's reasoning, their ability to think, or their personality? Suppose that you had a ray gun and that with it you could aim a beam at Hitler's head and in a flash turn him into what is sometimes unkindly called a human vegetable. Suppose that with the push of a button you could destroy his mind. That wouldn't be killing him because we're imagining that after the ray takes effect Hitler continues to live but is unable to pursue his plans for world domination. He's helpless, and we've saved millions of lives and prevented all the suffering that we know historically Hitler ultimately produced. Would that be okay? Are we then still acting in accord with your moral principle that all human life is sacred? Or do you really mean something more than the mere biological life and organic functioning of a human being?

C: I see where this is leading . . .

P: I hope so. Because the next question is whether in the case of horrible crimes committed within a society it would be morally justified on your principle that all human life is sacred to destroy the minds while preserving the living bodies of capital criminals. We needn't actually execute them in that case. We could just erase enough of their cognitive functioning so that they would never again have enough psychological capability to commit another crime. We take care of their bodies, keep them nourished and reasonably protected from disease, and so on, until they die of natural causes. Would that satisfy your desire not to bring about the death even of the worst criminals around us? Would we be acting morally by punishing criminals if we could painlessly destroy their minds?

C: That is a very strange suggestion. I'll have to think about this for a while before I can answer. I'm tempted to say on the one hand that if we destroy a person's mind, then we have in fact killed him or her as a human being. Even if their body continues to function biologically, we will have decided to destroy the person they once were.

P: Yes. That's what I'm asking you to consider. I want to know on the basis of your answer exactly what you mean when you say that all human *life* is sacred and exactly what you mean by *life* and *living* in this context.

C: It's an interesting case, I admit.

P: Would you find it to be a cruel and unusual punishment?

C: I don't know. I suppose, given our previous discussion, I can't really say that it's cruel if the procedure is painlessly done. And I suppose I can't really say that it's unusual if by that we just mean what is often or typically done in such cases. If many nations adopted the practice as a way of dealing with their criminals, or if, relative to a single society, it became the normal way of handling the deadliest wrongdoers, then I guess it wouldn't be unusual once the method was well established.

P: The "cruel" part seems to be the difficult concept. What's unusual is relative to what happens to occur, that is, unless the entire phrase "cruel and unusual punishment" is just another way of referring to torture.

C: Still, I think that you kill the person when you erase their mind. You destroy their personality, what makes them an individual thinking conscious human being.

P: Exactly. That's the point, you see. Because I'm trying to exert a little pressure on your slogan that you're opposed to capital punishment on the grounds that it involves playing God in violating the moral principle that all human life is sacred. You don't really mean human *life*, do you? You mean something more than merely living or merely being alive. You are interested in protecting a living human being's thoughts and personality, the *mind* rather than merely the *body* of a living human being. Isn't that it?

C: I'm interested in human dignity, in the moral right to life of every human being.

P: Then I think we might be finally bringing our deepest underlying differences to the surface. You seem to regard every human being as having an absolutely unconditional right to life, whereas I believe that the right to life of a human being is conditional on their showing equal respect for the moral right to life of others.

C: So, you think that you can lose the right to life on the basis of what you do, in your behavior toward others?

P: Yes, something like that. I don't think it's a very easy thing to jeopardize your right to life. You have to do something extremely drastic. Like the things we've been talking about, say, the man who raped, beat, and then buried alive that little nine-year-old girl in a pair of plastic garbage bags. He didn't treat her as though he had any conception whatsoever of her right to life. He used her to satisfy his selfish desires, and then he discarded her as though she was just so much rubbish to get rid of. He actually disposed of her while she was still alive in garbage bags. Now, I think that where moral rights are concerned, there has to be some reciprocation. If you don't have respect for the rights of others, then you forfeit your right to be treated with respect for any moral right to life yourself.

C: You're saying that you have to earn the right to life, that it doesn't just come automatically.

P: Not quite. I don't say that you have to *earn* the right. You start out with the right to life. But you can do certain extreme things by free choice whereby you can *lose* the right. If you have acted badly enough, deliberately in violation of another person's rights, then you are no longer entitled to have a right to life protected by others in your own case. Society is based on a kind of implicit contract. When you violate the terms of the contract, then you give up what you might otherwise have taken for granted as guaranteed by virtue of your participation in the social order. I'll respect anyone's right to life, if you prefer, the fact that their life is sacred, but only if they also respect other persons' moral right to life. If they don't do that, if they demonstrate by their conduct that they have no regard for the lives of others, then they are no longer keeping their part of the social contract, and they have sacrificed the moral right they could otherwise be presumed to have from birth. After that, the right to life no longer covers and protects them. They can be executed under death penalty provisions of the law if they are found guilty of a capital offense, exhausted all their appeals, and gone through the usual process to make sure that no mistake has been made in their conviction.

C: If I understand what you're saying, when someone violates the social contract in a particular way, then, by virtue of losing the inborn right to life, society is free to enforce the death penalty against the individual. Is that right?

P: Yes. With certain qualifications, of course.

C: I'm not sure I agree with your interpretation of moral rights as conditional on a person's conduct.

P: Why not?

C: Here are some examples. I think that persons in a society have a right to be told the truth and not be lied to. Don't you?

P: Yes, sure.

C: Well, if someone lies to you, do you think that they thereby sacrifice their moral right to have the truth told to them? Do you think that after you catch someone in a lie, afterward you are morally entitled to lie to them? Or do you think that as a general thing you're morally obligated always to tell the truth, even to someone who has repeatedly lied to you?

P: I suppose I believe that we're all morally bound always to the tell the truth, no matter whether or not another person has been honest and truthful to us.

C: So, a person doesn't lose the moral right to be dealt with truthfully by virtue of failing to respect the truth in communicating with others.

P: I agree.

C: Then it follows that the moral right to have people speak truthfully to you is not conditional.

P: Not necessarily . . .

C: Are you changing your mind?

P: No. But it doesn't yet follow from anything I've said so far that the moral right not to be lied to isn't conditional, only at most that the moral right isn't conditional on one's telling the truth in every instance oneself.

C: What else could it be conditional on? And wouldn't that be the perfect analogy, between losing the moral right to life conditionally on one's cold-bloodedly taking the life of another? You murder, you lose your moral right to life; you lie, you lose your moral right always to be told the truth. Or how about stealing? Do we think it's morally permissible to steal from thieves? Would it ever be morally right for us to steal from anyone, including thieves? Or isn't stealing just plain morally wrong, and everyone, regardless of how they behave, has a moral right not to have their property stolen?

P: There are important differences here that I think you're overlooking.

C: Like what?

P: First, you might be right that the moral right to be told the truth is not conditional on a person's always telling the truth. But that doesn't mean that the moral right to be told the truth and not to be lied to isn't conditional on something else.

C: You said that. Like what?

P: It could be conditional on something such as the use you make of the truth you've been told. If you're told the truth about something dangerous that should be kept secret and you violate the confidence, causing injury or even death to other persons, then perhaps you lose the moral right thereafter to be told the truth.

C: That wouldn't cause you to lose the moral right not to be lied to, only perhaps that you not be told everything that you can't be trusted not to divulge. For that matter, you might not have a moral right to be told everything or to have all interesting information shared with you in the first place.

P: Oh, I think we can easily describe a plausible set of circumstances in which the only way to withhold information from persons who have proved by their past behavior that they're not to be trusted with sensitive content is to tell them a lie.

C: What would be a situation of that kind?

P: Suppose that the question is whether I know something that the untrustworthy person has good grounds to believe I might know. Then if I don't say anything, that person can correctly infer that I must be withholding something and can use that information improperly.

C: Far-fetched, isn't it?

P: Even so, it makes the general point that the moral right always to be told the truth or never to be lied to could be conditional on one's conduct and in particular on the use that's made of the information communicated.

C: What else?

P: Second, even if you're right that there's an unconditional moral right never to be lied to or stolen from, it doesn't follow that all moral rights are unconditional. In particular, therefore, it doesn't follow that the moral right to life is unconditional.

C: I would think that if *any* moral right is unconditional, then the moral right to life is *certainly* unconditional.

P: That needs to be shown. Notice, however, that I'm not saying that if you commit murder, then any private individual has the right to murder you or to deny you your right to life. I'm saying that by committing an act of premeditated, so-called first-degree murder, you sacrifice your conditional moral right to life, after which the state or society or the appropriate legal and judicial institutions not only have the moral permission but also the moral obligation to punish your action by ending your life, hopefully in as painless and untraumatic a way as possible.

C: What, by contrast, would be a conditional moral right other than what you're saying is the conditional moral right to life?

P: I just gave you an example, where being told the truth and not lied to might be conditional on the use you make of what you're told.

C: I find that example controversial. What's a clear-cut case of a conditional moral right that you can forfeit by bad behavior?

P: How about the moral right to vote in an election? You can lose that if you've committed certain kinds of felonies.

C: That's a legal or social right, not a moral right. There can't be a moral right to vote because many societies aren't democratic and don't have an institution of voting, but moral rights extend to all societies regardless of their laws and practices.

P: You're right. Okay. Unless, of course, someone says that everyone really does have a moral right to participate in the government by which they are ruled and that societies that are not democratic and don't have an institution of voting are actually violating the people's moral rights. But if you don't like that example, then what about the moral right to go where you want and associate with whomever you want? That's not unconditional. Criminals who have been convicted of certain crimes when they're on parole are restricted in their movements and the persons with whom they can associate. In particular, parolees are not allowed to associate with known felons. They violate the condition on what is otherwise a moral right for everyone in every society, showing that the moral right in general is conditional on not having committed whatever crimes carry that penalty.

C: I'm not so sure that's a *moral* right . . .

P: Oh, come on. You want to say that it's not a moral right, other things being equal, to go where you want and spend time with whatever persons you want? Don't we all have that right unless we've done something to jeopardize it by our misconduct?

C: What if I said what you just answered about societies being morally unjust that don't recognize the rights of members to vote and participate democratically in their own governance?

P: Do you seriously want to say that a society that puts people in prison or imposes parole restrictions for antisocial behavior is inherently unjust? Do you want to claim that any punishment restricting the movement and social interaction of persons based on their conviction after due judicial procedure is automatically a violation of a person's unconditional moral rights?

C: I guess that would be going too far, wouldn't it?

P: Absolutely. More important, it would be inconsistent with your position that it is better to incarcerate capital offenders for life rather than executing them under a death penalty.

C: Point taken.

P: And here's another example. What about the moral right to freedom of speech or freedom of religion? Those moral rights, if you think they are moral rights, to say what you want and to worship as you choose, are also conditional on how you exercise them and on the content of what you express in exercising them. I would say that you give up the moral right to free speech if you persistently attempt to prevent other persons from exercising their moral right to free speech and similarly for the freedom of religion. For that matter, you can also sacrifice the moral right to freedom of religion by practicing religions that violate other persons' moral rights, as when a religion requires human sacrifice or even in the case of religious rituals involving the cruel mistreatment of animals.

C: I think I agree with most of what you've just said, but I'm not sure about the last part. You don't give up your moral right to worship as you please when you violate the rights of others or engage in other socially objectionable conduct. You still have the moral right; it's just that the moral right never included the right to human sacrifice or mistreatment of animals in the first place. You continue to have the right to worship in other ways, by not breaking other moral or social rules that involve especially violating the moral and legal rights of others.

P: Well, in that case, you're making my point that not all moral rights are unconditional. We don't have an absolutely unconditional moral right to free speech or freedom of religion. Rather, there are conditions that have to be observed, or else our exercise of such freedoms can be legitimately limited or punished by law.

C: Maybe you're right; maybe there are conditional moral rights. It still doesn't follow that the moral right to life is conditional. Besides, the mere fact, if it is a fact, that society is permitted to execute a criminal doesn't necessarily mean that it should do so or that society needs to make use of the death penalty.

P: That's right, I think. It's discretionary. After a criminal shows repeated disregard for the moral right to life of others, then society has the option of no longer regarding the criminal as having a moral right to life. Again, we're only talking about the most extreme types of crime and generally in the case of repeat offenders, though also with exceptions.

C: But if it's merely an option, then it doesn't follow that criminals who have demonstrated a disregard for the right to life of others should be executed.

P: The point is that at this stage of criminal proceedings, if my argument is correct, a society has the moral authority to execute a capital offender. You were previously questioning what could possibly give the criminal justice system the moral right to take another human being's life, and I say that society has that moral right when a criminal has shown complete disregard for the moral right to life of other human beings.

C: Would that also be true for your science fiction scenario where we could simply erase a criminal's mind without destroying their body, letting the body live on after the personality has been eliminated?

P: I suppose so, although I don't really see the point. If society has the right to end the life of individuals who have no respect for the right to life of others, then they might as well be executed. I was asking whether you would be satisfied to have such criminals' minds erased while preserving the life of their bodies since you were arguing specifically that there was a sacred, unconditional moral right to life that extends to every human being regardless of their conduct in society. I was wondering whether you were primarily interested in the moral right to *life*—and *life*, biologically speaking—as something sacred, or whether you had something more psychological in mind.

C: More psychological, I guess.

P: Good. So erasing someone's mind is out of the question for you, as far as you're concerned. It also constitutes a morally objectionable alternative to capital punishment.

C: I think it *is* capital punishment carried on in a somewhat different, unconventional way. If the personality is destroyed, then the person is effectively dead. The mere continuation of heartbeat, respiration, and other body functions, is irrelevant. The person in that state has been killed and is already dead.

P: I wonder if the opponents of euthanasia would necessarily agree with you.

C: Probably not, but I'm prepared to argue the point. I don't have any moral objections to euthanasia in the case of persons who are truly and finally brain-dead. They are permanently dead as persons, in the way that I would define the concept of a person, so there is no justification, unless it offers comfort to friends and family, to preserve the purely mechanical functioning of whatever is left of their bodies. The difficulty is always knowing in practice whether a person is truly, finally, and irrevocably brain-dead or whether it might not be possible at some later time for them to revive. That's where the moral difficulty comes in, I think. We're discussing things in the abstract as a thought experiment, where we can simply stipulate that the person is irrecoverably brain-dead. If we *know* that, then I think the person is gone for good and what happens to the body, beyond the normal respect we owe to the dead, doesn't really matter. The problem is that we don't and we can't always know this when we're faced with the question, say, of whether to shut down a life support system for a patient who appears to be permanently brain-dead.

P: We're together on that. However, what you've just brought up suggests a new twist, another variation on the thought experiment.

C: What's that?

P: Well, if part of your concern about the ethics of capital punishment is that when a criminal is executed there's no going back and correcting a mistaken conviction, what if we could, speaking science-fictionally again, *temporarily* erase the condemned's personality? We keep their bodies alive, and we leave open the option of restoring their minds. Then, if it later turns out that we've made a mistake and wrongly convicted them, we reinstate their personalities and free them.

C: That's a little too bizarre.

P: Why? It's no stranger than any of the other assumptions we've been entertaining. What I'm interested in are the conceptual implications for your view of the morally sacred right to life, where by "life" I understand you now to mean the life of the mind, the psychology and personality, memories, thoughts, expectations, experiences, and so on, of a human being. I would be satisfied, when a temporary erasure of personality is performed, that the condemned is "executed" in the sense that unless new information comes to light, someone guilty of a capital crime would be effectively, psychologically, dead. And you should, I would think, be satisfied that we haven't thereby done anything irreversible. We can always go back if we'd made a wrong judgment and restore the individual's mental life, after which we release them, body and soul, from prison.

C: I see what you're saying. So, if we had a ray gun, as you've imagined, or a magic cabinet or philosopher's pill, then at least my qualms about the irreversibility of the conventional death penalty ought to be overcome, while you'd still be satisfied, at least as I define the concept of "life" and "death" of a human being, as a discontinuation of mental faculties and personality, that a meaningful death sentence or capital punishment had finally been carried out. Is that it?

P: Yes. And, what's more, such a practice might even avoid complaints about lifelong incarceration without the possibility of parole as constituting cruel and unusual punishment. If we've erased a capital criminal's brain, not the brain itself, of course, but somehow caused it to temporarily cease functioning in such a way as to support all conscious thinking and personality, then the criminal wouldn't suffer the day-to-day misery of life in prison. We just warehouse their bodies in case evidence comes to light indicating that they were actually innocent. If it should turn out that they were wrongly convicted, then we restore their consciousness, and, if not, then we give their bodies a proper burial when they eventually die of natural causes.

C: Can we bring this discussion back down to earth?

P: It's just a thought experiment. Still, it's rather revelatory, don't you think? The problem helps bring out what we really think about the deeper moral issues involved in the death penalty by throwing off the usual practical constraints that limit the ways in which a society can actually deal with its worst criminal offenders.

C: But we don't live in a science fiction fantasy. We live in a real world of real practical constraints.

P: I'm trying to clarify so that I can more clearly understand the underlying principles of your objection to capital punishment. We can make those principles stand out more clearly in sharp relief if we ask what implications they would have if we could administer justice in different ways than are actually available to us in practice. Of course, when we're done, and we think we see what the principles are in a brighter light, then, you're right, we have to come back down to earth and apply those principles within the limitations of the technology and social realities that actually prevail.

C: Good. You had me worried there for a minute.

P: Before, you were asking about whether a criminal's violating the social contract by showing utter disregard for the moral right to life of others should give society the right to take their life. You wanted, and I suppose you still want to say, that the morally sacred right to personality and conscious mental life is absolutely unconditional, so that we cannot justifiably take it away even from the worst criminals among us who have no respect for the right to life of others.

C: Exactly.

P: Well, I would say that by violating the social contract in that extreme way, criminals do give up their own moral right to life and that their actions in such cases give society the moral right to deny them the continuation of their own lives. Since we don't have a magic ray gun, cabinet, or philosopher's pill, then that means in real practice that society has the moral right to execute them.

C: What I was saying was that having the right to execute a criminal doesn't make it necessary. It doesn't imply that a criminal should be executed.

P: And, again, I regard that option as discretionary on the part of society. What I was trying to do was to clear away your objection that on ethical grounds society can never have the moral right and hence never have the option to execute its worst criminal offenders. I'm claiming that such a right does exist when criminals forfeit their own moral right to life by failing to respect the moral right to life of others.

C: Then, what additionally is required to justify the actual enforcement of capital punishment for a particular crime?

P: I would say that your question is answered by considerations of justice. Justice in certain cases requires that persons pay for their extreme crimes by having the state bring an end to their lives.

C: Justice?

P: Yes, justice. You've seen representations of justice personified as a goddess wearing a blindfold and holding a pair of scales, haven't you?

C: Frequently.

P: The blindfold symbolizes the ideal that justice should be "blind" in the sense that the law must apply equally and impartially to all persons, regardless of their circumstances.

C: I agree.

P: The scales or balance pans is the part of the image that I'm especially interested in, however. What they signify to me is that justice must weigh its penalties and rewards, but especially its penalties, against the actions for which the penalties are assigned. The scales would be tipped way out of proportion, for example, if, under current economic conditions, you were required by law to pay a trillion dollars for a parking fine. Similarly, just to take another example to make the same point, if a court were to decide that you had to pay only fifteen cents for killing your entire family.

That wouldn't be justice because there wouldn't be an appropriate balance in the scales the goddess carries measuring what you've done against the punishment meted out for your offense.

C: Fair enough. Although I thought that the scale or balance pans were for weighing evidence in deciding who's guilty and who's innocent, the cases made by the prosecution and the defense.

P: It might be for that too, but justice obviously concerns sentencing as well. It's not up to justice to decide the facts of a trial, only to administer the requirements of law once the facts are decided. Now, I say that if a person has committed what is generally called a capital offense, such as willful cold-blooded premeditated first-degree murder, among other extreme crimes, then the only way for the scales of justice to balance is for the murderer also to lose his or her own life. That is what I mean by saying that justice demands the death penalty for those kinds of crimes. There's no other way to set a punishment so that it corresponds with what a person has done in taking another innocent life.

C: If I'm following you, then you're saying, first, that the violation of the social contract by a criminal's failing to respect the moral right to life of another gives society the moral authority through judicial processes to end the criminal's life and that, having assumed that moral authority, the demands of justice dictate that the only way to pay for such a horrible crime with an appropriate punishment is for the criminal to be executed, to lose his or her own life in payment for the crime. Anything less just isn't enough for justice to be done in the case of murder and other crimes of similar magnitude.

P: Roughly, yes.

C: Are you sure of that? I mean, how do you know? Why isn't it enough for the scales to balance if a murderer spends the rest of his or her life in prison?

P: This gets us finally to the question you were asking yesterday that I suggested we put off until today. Here's what I think. Put in one of the pans of the scale the fact that murdered persons have had their lives finally and permanently terminated. They are dead, never to return. They do not get to experience the good and bad days that all the rest of us get to experience. And they are dead not because an accident or some fatal disease has cut them down but because another person has chosen to end their lives. What can we put in the other side of the balance pans that will bring the scale into equal measure so that, as I believe justice demands, the punishment is proportionate to the crime? What payment will compensate society for the loss of one of its innocent contributors? If the criminal spends the rest of his or her life in prison, then the criminal still has good and bad days. A convict incarcerated for life has the opportunity to learn things, to reflect on the meaning of life, to enter into at least limited kinds of social relations within and outside prison, to develop artistic talents, and so on and to still be part of the world, all of which ordinary pleasures and pains of life they have completely deprived their victims of ever experiencing again. They live, even if only in prison, while their victims have been permanently robbed of their lives.

C: I take your point.

P: So, I ask, What can you possibly put in the scale that will bring the pans into balance when a person has unlawfully taken another person's life? There's no amount of money, no physical torment or deprivation, no time spent out of circulation within society by being imprisoned that can possibly repay what the capital offender has taken away from the person he or she has killed. And that's not to mention the loss to the family and friends, if the victim has any, and to society at large. Life in prison just isn't enough. We do not satisfy the requirements of justice, symbolized by the blindfolded goddess holding the scales, when we hand down any lesser sentence than the death penalty for those who have willingly caused the premeditated death of another. Nothing else evens out the scales or brings them into alignment.

C: Well, so what?

P: So what?

C: Yeah. So what if you're right that nothing else satisfies the requirements of justice? What's so important about making sure that justice has been served? What good does it do? It doesn't bring the victim back. It doesn't change anything. Justice is just an abstract concept. Why should anyone care whether justice is done?

P: Well, don't you think, as I do, that without the meaningful pursuit of justice, society would break down? I would say that to whatever extent the interests of justice are not served or are only imperfectly served, to that extent society suffers a loss of all the potential greatness that could be achieved for the happiness and betterment of all its members.

C: Maybe, maybe not.

P: If you're not concerned about the abstract interests of justice being served, then why do you care, as you've repeatedly indicated you do, about whether someone has been unjustly sentenced to death under a system of capital punishment? Why does it matter to you except as an act of injustice that a criminal might be executed for a crime that he or she didn't actually commit? Because, you see, I'm 100 percent with you in deploring the fact that some people are wrongly indicted, wrongly convicted, and wrongly sentenced and punished. I don't want anyone anywhere to even have to defend themselves at public expense for a crime they didn't actually commit, let alone to suffer a penalty when in fact they are innocent. That to me is just as morally objectionable a violation of their rights and of the fundamental principles of justice as when a capital offender does not pay a sufficient price for the crimes he or she commits.

C: You're right, I think, that justice is an important value after all. But I still say that executing a murderer doesn't bring the victim back. It only perpetuates the cycle of violence, whether an individual does the killing or the state. In fact, there's something particularly macabre and menacing about the anonymous machinery of a state execution. It's all too impersonal.

P: If that's true, as you say, then why put the murderer in prison at all? That doesn't bring the victim back either.

C: True.

P: And aren't the workings of the justice system generally rather impersonal? Isn't that partly the point? There's nothing personal or vindictive or vengeful going on; it's just administering to convicted criminals whatever punishments they've been sentenced to serve. Being processed into prison to serve a week or a lifetime sentence or to be executed for a capital crime, there's no animus involved. Or there shouldn't be, anyway. It's just the wheels of justice grinding away as they're meant to do when things function properly.

C: The difference is the finality of it, being led to your death by such a cold calculating set of procedures.

P: Don't forget that it's a punishment, the most severe punishment that a society can impose on what it deems to be its very worst criminals.

C: And if a mistake is made?

P: It's tragic, I agree, and we should do whatever we can to make sure it doesn't happen. But if we don't punish persons who have no regard for the moral right to life of others by depriving them of their own lives, then we are not fully serving the interests of justice. I've made the argument several times already, but I don't mind repeating myself: What if a wrongly sentenced person dies of natural causes while serving a life sentence in prison? We can't take that back either. The practical exercise of justice is always going to be imperfect. But if we don't try to measure up to the ideal of justice to the best of our abilities, then we aren't living as part of a truly law-abiding society that aspires to justice as a social ideal. The scales have to be in balance. The willful desecration of a life can be paid for in only one way—when the murderer is also deprived of life.

C: And yet there is a difference. If someone dies of natural causes while serving a life sentence, then the government has not taken on itself to end the prisoner's life. That's what it does when it carries out the death penalty. The prisoner would not have died in those circumstances unless a chain of events is initiated and followed through by representatives of the legal system. The person must be physically brought to an execution chamber, and the mechanism of execution must be applied. The state in that case *does* something; it *acts* so as to bring about the prisoner's death, which otherwise would not have occurred at just that place and time. It also willfully kills. And willfully to kill strikes me as inherently morally wrong, no matter what.

P: Do we need to go over all this territory again? You're talking about ending the consciousness of a human being, yes? We're not worried about plants or lower animals or cancerous human tissue. We're leaving entirely out of account the killing that is done in a just war, if there is such a thing. You mean, all those situations aside, that you think it's wrong deliberately to kill another human being in the specific sense of ending their consciousness. Is that right? And you mean, under no circumstances, as an absolute moral imperative, something that can never be violated no matter what, as you put it earlier, unconditionally.

C: Yes, that's what I mean.

P: You've never answered my question about killing in a just war.

C: That's slightly different. I consider that by extension to be the same as killing in self-defense. There's no self-defense justification for executing a prisoner once the person is securely in custody.

P: And what about my argument concerning the requirements of justice? How do we exactly balance the scales when someone has willfully taken another person's life?

C: I don't think that a murderer or anyone else in society can ever balance those scales because I think there's no way to make up for the loss of an innocent life. As a result, now that I've had more chance to think about it, I think I want to say that if we can't actually pay for the loss of life caused by murder, then there's no point in trying to do so by executing anyone convicted of the killing. We're only fooling ourselves if we think that by such an action we are balancing the scales of justice. We can't do that no matter what we do or how hard we try. So, we should concentrate instead on what we can meaningfully do with respect to the treatment of criminals within a humane, enlightened justice system.

P: Which for you is to imprison them for life without the possibility of parole?

C: When the circumstances warrant it, for repeat offenders and with aggravating circumstances in the commission of a premeditated first-degree murder, yes.

P: So, your feeling is that if you can't exactly balance the scales by having, say, a convicted serial killer pay for the crime with his or her own life, then we shouldn't try at all? Because I would say that despite the fact that we can't ever compensate for the loss of innocent life, we should try to approach the ideal as closely as we can and that we approach the ideal of a perfect balance of crime and punishment more closely by exacting from the worst criminals in our society the ultimate penalty in a carefully safeguarded judicious application of capital punishment.

C: I understand that's your view. My objections to it are that the ideal is fictional in the first place and that we don't contribute to the better good of society by executing capital offenders. Also, as I've tried to emphasize, the process, once carried out, is irrevocable, irreversible, and that poses problems also about trying even remotely to approximate an ideal of justice.

P: We are fully in agreement that mistakes of any kind in the justice system are unacceptable. Still, I think we owe it to the victims of the most terrible crimes to make those who have been found guilty of them pay the highest possible price. As a society, we thereby rid ourselves of persons who cannot control their violent behavior, and we make an important statement that we value the lives of the victims of capital criminals so highly that we are prepared to administer the most severe punishment available. We should make every effort to avoid bad sentencing, needless to say. If we shrink from taking this extreme kind of action in protecting society from persons who engage in extreme lawbreaking, who pose a serious threat to everyone's life, welfare, and happiness, then we are not doing our duty, and we are falling too far short of what justice demands of its responsible, law-abiding members.

C: And when we get things wrong? We know it happens, and we can be sure that innocent persons are waiting on death row in prisons throughout the country and throughout the world right now. Those innocent persons will die if the death penalty is allowed to remain in force. What about the requirements of justice with respect to innocent victims of the justice system itself? What about our responsibility as members of an enlightened, progressive society to set the proper moral and legal tone for other nations who are still engaged in the barbaric practices of capital punishment?

P: That's just rhetoric.

C: In response to yours . . .

P: Then let's return to your argument. Do you really want to say that from a moral perspective we should never undertake any action that might be irreversible with respect to mistakenly ending the life of an innocent person?

C: Maybe. But I sense a trap here.

P: No trap, just trying to clarify what your position is and what general moral principle you're invoking.

C: Then, let's say, for the sake of argument, at least for the time being, that you're interpreting my commitments correctly.

P: If so, then I think you've got some problems in trying to generalize that ethical stance with respect to all decision making.

C: How so?

P: Here's one difficulty. What about the physician who tries an experimental new drug or surgical procedure on a terminally ill patient? If the physician makes a mistake and the patient dies, then the decision is irreversible. But if the physician, inhibited by your moral principle, refrains from undertaking the new treatment, then the patient is deprived of a possible cure. There are risks in everything. If we don't take such risks, we also sacrifice potential benefits. Failing to take full advantage of those potential benefits in certain cases because we're afraid of doing something irreversible with respect to the lives of innocent persons merely on the grounds that we might make a mistake in judgment can also be a violation of our moral obligations. What do you say to that?

C: There are obvious differences. The physician *might* accidentally cause the death of an innocent person if the drugs or procedure don't work properly, but the execution of someone condemned to death is virtually guaranteed to do so. It's not only irreversible, it's inevitable. And it's intended to be. Even if the execution equipment fails to function properly, the prison will just try again until the sentence is carried out. That's as close to certain death as we can imagine in the world of practical affairs. The doctor case is not the same since the doctor is not trying to kill the patient but, on the contrary, trying to save the patient. If things go wrong, then the doctor fails, and an innocent person is accidentally killed. In the case of capital punishment, the purpose and intention is to kill, and there's virtually no chance that a mistake will result in the condemned person, guilty or innocent, somehow completely escaping death.

P: I think you're looking at the analogy in the wrong way.

C: What do you mean?

P: The purpose of the death penalty is not only or even primarily to kill a person, let alone an innocent person. The purpose is to enforce a certain standard of justice. If you like, the analogy might be extended to say that the death penalty is a procedure adopted by a state as a way of protecting and curing itself of a particular sort of social ailment, the existence of individuals who are destructive to society as a whole. I'm not entirely satisfied with this way of putting things, but you might try to imagine the death penalty as something like extreme surgery to remove a cancerous tumor from the body politic.

Left to itself, unpunished or insufficiently punished criminal behavior threatens to destroy society, just as an untreated disease might do in the case of the health of an individual human body. What counts as a mistake in the analogy is therefore not failing to execute a prisoner but accidentally executing an innocent person who has gone through the whole legal process and been wrongfully convicted. I admit that that kind of thing can happen and that we should exercise every effort and spare no expense to make sure it doesn't. But I think you can't reasonably say that the physician analogy is faulty because the physician is trying to save a life and the institution of capital punishment is trying to kill or cause death or the loss of life, let alone of innocent life. The death penalty similarly has as its purpose saving the life of society at large, protecting society from destructive forces at loose within it, and in that sense trying to save the "life" of the social structure.

C: That's still a big difference, shifting from what happens to an individual under a physician's care to what happens to society as a whole, made up of indefinitely many individual persons.

P: You're right, of course. But that's how I meant the analogy to be understood. It's also the sense in which I wanted to consider how mistakes can occur in both the practice of the physician and the machinery connected with the death penalty that can result in both cases in the accidental loss of innocent life. I wouldn't say, and I wonder now if you still would and still want to say that because there is a chance that things can go wrong and mistakes can be made, we shouldn't try to do what physicians and the justice system implementing the death penalty are designed and intended to do. That is, to help cure and preserve the health of an individual and the "health," analogically understood, of society as a whole made up of many individuals. Should we be so afraid of the possibility of error that we don't even try to do what justice requires?

C: We're speaking hypothetically about the lives of innocent persons. And this is not sheer fantasy since we know that innocent persons have been executed.

P: Regrettably true. By the same token, we know that patients, also hypothetically considered as innocent individuals, under a physician's care, have sometimes lost their lives through mistaken diagnoses and failed experimental methods of healing. Does that mean that no physician, in keeping with your general moral principle, should ever attempt any potentially risky procedure that might accidentally lead to a patient's death, just because something unfortunate might happen?

C: You still don't see the differences here?

P: There must be differences. Every analogy also has disanalogies; otherwise, the things being compared would simply be identical. The question is whether the disanalogies significantly outweigh the analogies in a relevant respect. We say that an orange is analogous to planet Earth, for example, in being round, having a surface and an interior core, and things like that; but we're not going to mistake one for the other, and we're not going to disallow the analogy on the grounds that there are obvious disanalogies.

C: Well, here's a crucial, and I'm already beginning to think decisive, disanalogy between your two cases. You say that a physician treating a patient experimentally might make mistakes ending an innocent person's life and that the state administering capital punishment is like a physician to the body politic, which might also make mistakes resulting in the occasional but hopefully rare death of an innocent person. Have I got it?

P: Exactly.

C: Then I object by pointing out that when a physician is pressed to try potentially dangerous experimental methods of curing a patient, there really is, practically speaking, no good alternative. The physician and patient alike are up against it. If they don't try something desperate, the physician's professional opinion is that the patient will definitely die, perhaps in a rather short period of time. As a heroic measure, the physician then decides with all due hesitation and reflection to attempt to save the patient's life by some new and relatively unproven technique. If it succeeds, perfect; if not, the patient was going to die soon anyway. That's simply not the case with respect to society and an executioner's acting as a kind of physician to try to cure society of its ills. Society as a whole is not about to perish just because we decide that it is more ethical to imprison our worst criminal offenders for life without the possibility of parole as opposed to putting them very permanently to death. So, as I've said several times now, there's no necessity to implementing a death penalty. We keep the most serious wrongdoers under lock and key for the rest of their lives so that they can't injure others, and we avoid the moral taint of killing other human beings under sanction of the state. We avoid any possibility of irreversibly terminating persons who might later turn out to have been innocent, wrongly accused, convicted, sentenced, and executed. We thereby dramatically increase the likelihood that we can undo a judicial mistake that is otherwise impossible to correct. We won't have done anything that absolutely can't be fixed.

P: Unless the wrongly convicted person dies of natural causes while imprisoned.

C: I only said that we significantly increase the chances of not violating an innocent person's right to life. And you agree with me, I think, that innocent persons have an undeniable, even if conditional, as you would have it, right to life. I don't agree that the right to life is conditional. But I'm saying that, even on your concept of a conditional right to life, innocent, wrongly convicted persons waiting for execution on death row, have a moral right to life. They haven't actually done anything that would or should cause them to relinquish their moral right to life. We're supposing that they're innocent of the crimes for which they've been mistakenly sentenced to death.

P: That's right. They're innocent, and as such they have an untarnished but still conditional right to life in my opinion. And we should do everything in our power within reason to make sure that they are not accidentally wrongfully executed or, for that matter, punished in any morally objectionable way, by the judicial system.

C: If we're agreed about all that, then why are you hesitating to accept my conclusion that the best, morally most defensible policy decision for a just, enlightened, and progressive society is not to execute even its worst criminals but to incarcerate them indefinitely unless subsequent developments prove them to have been mistakenly convicted? Then we can rescue them from the nightmare of having been caught up in the gears of the judicial machinery and restore them to their proper role as law-abiding members of society, even compensating them for the life-shattering trouble to which they have been subjected through no fault of their own.

P: I agree that all of those possibilities are advantages of your approach. However, I think that you're missing the bigger picture. In the first place, I don't think it's right to say that society is not in mortal danger from its worst criminals. I think you underestimate the extent to which we are all put at risk by unpunished or inadequately punished capital offenses. You say that this is a disanalogy with the physician who is driven to extreme experimental measures in order to save a patient's life, but I think first of all that the analogy is quite exact on precisely this pivotal point.

C: By the way, I wish you wouldn't refer to these categories of crimes as "capital" offenses. They're only capital crimes if we assume that a system of capital punishment is in place or should be in place, that it's justified to execute criminals who commit these kinds of crimes.

P: Point taken. But I think you know what I mean. I'm talking about the caliber of crimes that would be punished—and that I think ought to be punished—by the death penalty. These are crimes, whichever ones if any we decide they are, that would qualify those properly tried, convicted, and sentenced to humane execution, if a system of capital punishment were not only socially instituted but morally justified. That's what I mean by capital crimes.

C: Okay. Just as long as you don't lose track of the fact that you're invoking an enormous "if" and that I don't agree that there are any such crimes, none whatsoever.

P: Alright. So, we disagree about whether and to what extent our society is at risk by the existence of dangerous criminals unless we implement a death penalty.

C: To me, that's precisely where your analogy breaks down.

P: Would you agree, though, that if you were diagnosed with cancer, even if you weren't immediately at risk of dying, that you would accept your physician's professional advice about what to do after early detection of the disease to make sure that it doesn't spread and get worse? Would you also agree that, if, for a particular type of disease, there were no other method of cure available, you would consider it not only expedient but actually obligatory on your part in preserving your health to stop the cancer in its tracks while you still can?

C: I guess so. It depends. What are the real odds that the disease will get worse? And what are the risks associated with experimental methods that haven't yet proved effective?

P: Suppose that the disease is well enough understood from other patients' prognoses that if you don't act in a sufficiently timely fashion, as early in the progress of the disease as possible, the disease will relatively quickly gain hold of your health, after which it will be virtually impossible to eradicate. As for the risks of the experimental methods that your physician might recommend, let them be the same as whatever you took them to be in our previous discussion of the analogy.

C: Then I imagine that I would want the best available professionally recommended care that offered the best chances of defeating the disease as early as possible. I agree that where these kinds of sicknesses are concerned, the earlier the detection and the earlier we prevent the disease from gaining ground, the better off we are, the more likely we are of surviving.

P: Good. Well, that's what I say about curbing the spread of what I'm calling capital offenses in a society. The sooner and most decisively we cut them off, the better are society's chances of surviving with its values intact. Let me put the problem this way. If by instituting a death penalty we cause even one potential criminal to decide against committing a capital offense against an innocent victim, then the death penalty in my opinion is fully morally justified.

C: Even if mistakes are made along the way?

P: We'll minimize those to the point of insignificance by having plenty of checks and balances on the system, together with opportunities for open appeal, and maximum use of all the methods of modern forensic science. We don't want any innocent person to be executed, but equally we don't want any guilty person not to be held to the absolute requirements of justice in balancing the scales by relinquishing their own life for any innocent life taken. If we don't nip this social cancer in the bud, I'm convinced it can quickly grow out of control, and then, too late, society will be fighting for its survival after it's become extremely difficult once again to gain the upper hand.

C: What you haven't convinced me of yet is that society is really in that kind of danger from what you're calling capital criminals. I don't sense that level of threat. If you ask me whether I'd feel differently if it were my own family or friends who were to become the victims of crime, then I'd answer honestly that I obviously wouldn't want it to happen and that I might even feel a desire for revenge against those who have taken away something so precious from me. But we're deciding these issues not on the basis of emotions and gut reactions but by applying reason and what the best arguments tell us we should follow as public policy in as emotionally indifferent a way as possible. I am trying to abstract my thinking from what I might feel, and, in any case, I don't have any clear idea in advance of what I might or might not feel under those almost unthinkable circumstances.

P: I don't think I have any clear sense of how I'd feel either. And I don't ask you to consider these issues from the standpoint of feeling.

C: We're not making progress, are we?

P: That depends on what you mean by and what you expect from progress. I think we're clarifying our reasons for and against the death penalty, and that counts as progress in my book. Some of our arguments have come around in different versions, but the mere fact that they resurface in different ways in response to different kinds of challenges also tells us something interesting about how we're thinking about these things. It doesn't seem to me that we're just repeating ourselves because we're offering new arguments and seeing our positions reflected in light of different kinds of challenges. On the other hand, I do think that we have largely defined our respective outlooks fairly sharply at this point, and I don't think that either one of us is at any risk of simply giving in to the other. Speaking for myself, I'm not ready to capitulate and say that the death penalty ought to be abolished for any of the reasons you've articulated so far. You haven't convinced me of anything yet, and I don't think I've convinced you of anything either, have I?

C: No. Definitely not.

3

⚜

Day Three:
Conditional versus
Unconditional Right to Life

MORNING DRIVE

The two friends are taking a road trip. Driving together to a neighboring city to attend the opening of a new modern art exhibit, C and P are accompanied by S, who, as it happens, is completing a degree in criminal justice studies. They take turns at the wheel, and while en route the conversation naturally turns to the topic that has preoccupied P and C for the previous two days. S, as soon appears, has a wealth of practical information about death penalty practices and related statistics worldwide but does not have any firm convictions about whether capital punishment is morally right or wrong and does not entirely share P's and C's enthusiasm for philosophical discussion.

C: There's the turnoff.

P: I see it.

S: Thanks for inviting me along. I saw this show advertised in the law school bulletin, but I didn't think I'd have a chance to go.

C: Our pleasure. My dad let me borrow the family car.

S: You two seem strangely quiet. It's not like you to go this long without having something to say.

P: We've been talking ourselves hoarse over the last two days.

C: That's right. And we don't seem to be making much progress. I can't convince P, and P can't convince me.

S: About what?

C: About whether the death penalty is morally acceptable. P says yes, I say no. but we can't seem to break through one another's bedrock commitments. P thinks that justice requires the death penalty, in something like a modified eye-for-an-eye, tooth-for-a-tooth mentality.

P: That's a gross oversimplification and distortion.

C: Something like that, anyway. And I think it's morally wrong for the state ever to end a person's life if there's any other way of meeting its obligation to preserve order and administer the law. I'm in favor of prison sentences without possibility of parole in the case of the most serious lawbreakers in society, serial killers and terrorists, for example. And I'm concerned about the fact that if we execute someone, then we have no way of reversing the harm we've done if it turns out later that the person was innocent. I think that true justice requires that we never deliberately take an irreversible step with respect to the treatment of criminals and that the death penalty is about as irreversible a punishment as there could possibly be.

S: I see.

P: I'm not sure you want to get mixed up in this.

S: No, I'm interested. And I've been researching some of the background to the administration of capital punishment not only in the United States but elsewhere in the world.

C: Do you mean you've brought that stuff along?

P: That's quite a portable archive you've got set up in the backseat.

S: I need to work on the files this weekend, and I'm compiling a couple of summaries of the information for my boss to use.

C: Well, I wish you'd share what you know because we've been mostly arguing in a vacuum so far. We have a general sense of what the figures are, but it would be good to have some concrete evidence if we're ever going to move the discussion along.

P: That's what I think too. You won't need to chip in for gas if you can help settle some of the disputes we've been having.

S: Good deal. But all I've got are facts. I'm not much in the way of opinions. In fact, I've been collecting information all this semester for my sociology professor, who has funding for a project comparing the death penalty law in a number of different countries.

C: Perfect. So, if we have questions, can you tell us what you know?

S: Absolutely.

P: Here's something I'd like to learn. How many persons have been executed in the history of the United States? How many are on death row now awaiting execution?

S: I've got something on that. Let me see . . .

P: If you don't have stats on the entire history of the United States, what about the past several years on average?

C: Also, what is the capital punishment situation in the rest of the world? How many countries have the death penalty, how many have outlawed it, and how recently?

S: Hold on . . .

P: Where does your information come from?

S: Yeah, yeah. Give me a minute . . .

C: Take your time.

S: Okay. Here's one report that comes from a nonprofit organization called Death Penalty Focus. They have brochures and newsletters and a website. They seem to be mostly California based, but they have chapters all over, and they keep statistics for the entire United States. This is what they say about themselves: "We believe that the death penalty is an ineffective, cruel, and simplistic response to the serious and complex problem of violent crime. It institutionalizes discrimination against the poor and people of color, diverts attention and financial resources away from preventative measures that would actually increase public safety, risks the execution of innocent people, and does not deter crime. We are convinced that when the electorate is informed about the true human and financial costs associated with state-sanctioned killing, the United States will join the majority of nations throughout the world who have abolished it. Death Penalty Focus has eleven active volunteer chapters in California and more than 10,000 members nationwide."

C: That sounds like a useful place to start.

P: I'm sure their statistics will turn out to be accurate as far as they go, but you can hardly describe them as an impartial, unbiased information source. Clearly, they've got an ax to grind in their effort to abolish the death penalty in the United States.

C: It doesn't mean their facts aren't correct.

P: No, I don't suggest that. I just think that we need to scrutinize what they say with some care and try to compare it with information from other sources that either have no stake in the debate over capital punishment or represent another side of the issue.

S: Anyway, here's what they say in a report from 2007 containing information gathered from an NAACP (National Association for the Advancement of Colored People) report titled "Death Row USA." Nationwide, at that time, there were 3,309 men and 57 women on death row, for a total of 3,366. Of those, by racial distribution, 1,525 were White, 1,407 Black, 356 Hispanic, 38 Native American, and 39 Asian in racial origin. The total number of executions in the United States in a thirty-year period from 1976 through November 2006 was 1,048 men and 11 women, for a total of 1,059.

P: Interesting. Now, what do we infer from this?

C: It looks at first as though there's virtually no racial discrimination between Blacks and Whites in death penalty sentencing since there's a difference in absolute numerical terms of only 118, and there are more Whites than Blacks on death row. But just think about it. Blacks, African Americans, make up only about 11 percent of the total population in the United States, roughly the same as the number of Hispanics and Asians combined, although those numbers are changing. So that means that although Blacks represent only 11 percent of the U.S. population, they account for—let me punch these numbers in on my calculator—almost 42 percent of the number of persons sentenced to death at the time these statistics were compiled.

P: Right. And what do you infer from *that*?

C: Well, first, I would say this proves that there's a definite racial prejudice built into the capital punishment system.

P: Whoa . . . how does it prove *that*?

C: I just told you that whereas Blacks represent only about 11 percent of the U.S. population, they make up almost 42 percent, approaching one-half of the number of persons awaiting execution on death row.

S: That's useful for my research. What about the other racial categories?

C: It looks as though Hispanics represent less than 11 percent of those sentenced to death, Native Americans just over 1 percent and Asians also just over 1 percent.

P: Look, I agree that there's lots of discrimination still today against racial minorities in the United States and especially against African Americans. But I don't see how those statistics show that there's something inherently racially discriminatory about the death penalty and how it's administered by the American justice system.

C: Are you kidding?

P: S, don't you have anything to add here?

S: I'm just enjoying the ride and the conversation. And I'm happy to dig out more information whenever you need it. I'll look around myself and see what I can find.

P: Well, I think what you'd need in order to prove that capital punishment in the United States is racially prejudicial is something more substantial than these bare statistics.

C: Like what?

P: For starters, you'd need to ask whether, for whatever individual or social reasons, Blacks, percentage-wise, relative to the total population base, happen to commit more capital crimes than Whites. If they do, and if they're caught and convicted, then the fact that percentage-wise, relative again to the total population base, there happen to be more Blacks than Whites serving time on death row does not imply that they're being discriminated against on the basis of color.

C: We all know that Blacks are at a distinct disadvantage when they enter the legal system because they are often economically underprivileged and that also, because of many decades of racial discrimination, at least historically, many have been undereducated. Persons with those social disadvantages are unlikely to be represented by truly competent and committed lawyers, and they wind up getting more severe sentences, including the death penalty when it applies. And that's not even to mention the racial prejudice of some judges and juries.

P: You may be right, but I still say that these statistics just as S has reported them don't contain enough information to be able to draw those conclusions with any assurance.

C: What more do you want? What more do you need?

P: I'd like to know, first of all, whether and in what percentage Blacks as opposed to Whites and other racial categories of prisoners have been *wrongly* sentenced to death. If you could demonstrate that a disproportionate number of Blacks have been denied due process or have received mistaken sentences, then I think we would have clear evidence that the justice system is seriously flawed when it comes to handing out punishments for serious crimes. I think I agree, from lots of anecdotal sources, that Blacks probably are at a disadvantage in the legal system or at least that historically they have been. I'm furious when I see on television that Blacks are randomly stopped by police more often than members of other racial groups when they're out driving especially in largely White neighborhoods. I detest hate crimes of any sort, and I don't want to have any persons trying to live their lives within the law subjected to any kind of harassment. I don't want there to be mistreatment of any persons, regardless of color or gender, religion, sexual orientation, or whatever, either by private individuals and most certainly not by the police.

S: Then, why don't you agree with C?

P: I just don't think we've got enough of the right kinds of evidence here logically to conclude that racial distributions on death row constitute proof of discrimination in the administration of the death penalty. Maybe there is; probably there is, relying again on general impressions and anecdotal information that just seems to be in the airwaves within our culture. But so far these statistics don't fully make the case.

C: You want more data, more scientific study.

P: If we're going to make policy decisions affecting the lives and deaths of individuals in our society on the basis of statistical information, then, yes, I think we need to be very careful in drawing inferences from the data we have, and we need to make sure that we are not jumping to conclusions when we confront facts like these about who is and who isn't on death row. We need to dig deeper and try to understand what these statistics really mean in order to find out why certain percentages of individuals have a higher or lower presence in a particular sociological category.

C: I see what you mean. S, do you have anything more?

S: I'm looking . . .

P: For example. You notice that there are 3,309 men on death row in 2006, is that the figure? And, if I remember rightly, only 57 women.

S: Correct.

P: So, do the arithmetic again. It looks like that means that about 98 percent of death row prisoners are male and only 2 percent female.

C: That's right.

P: But you're not going to argue that the justice system in administering the death penalty is inherently discriminatory against men, are you? Or that the law is prejudiced in favor of women? No. You'll say that men commit more dangerous crimes than women, and these facts are reflected, as we would expect them to be, in the death row statistics.

C: I see.

P: Good. This doesn't have anything essentially to do with righting the wrongs in our society or trying to cover them up or ignore them or making up for prejudicial behavior by a racial majority against a racial minority in the past. It has to do first and foremost with how we should read and interpret the statistical data and what meaning we can attach to it if we are trying to use sociological science in shaping public policy. The first thing we have to do is look behind the statistics to try to understand what they mean. If I can put it this way, continuing the physician and healing of individuals and society analogy that C and I were exploring yesterday, then I would say that statistics are only a symptom, not a cause, of social problems. We have to search beyond the symptoms to try to understand and cure whatever it is that's causing the disease.

C: Well, the cause of persons being on death row is the fact that we have a death penalty. No death penalty, no statistics about people being on death row.

P: Very true, but also very unhelpful. It might be that, statistically speaking, relative to their population base, Blacks commit more dangerous crimes than Whites, just like men commit more dangerous crimes than women. It might be that there's a deep racial prejudice nationwide embedded in the criminal justice system that places Blacks at a disadvantage in being charged, convicted, and sentenced for dangerous crimes. It might be that the criminal justice system is fair as far as it goes but that Blacks are or at least historically have been at economic and educational disadvantages when it comes to getting adequate legal counsel when they're accused of crimes that can carry the death penalty. I don't know the answer to any of those questions just hearing about these statistics. And we need to know the reasons why the statistics are as they are if we're going to do something meaningful for the improvement of society and for the life of every member of society, regardless of their sociological category.

C: So, would it help also to know what the statistics say about how many Whites versus Blacks who are convicted of capital crimes are actually sentenced to death?

P: Oh, absolutely. That would be especially vital information because it would tell us what happens to persons in different racial groups once they have actually been found guilty of a crime that involves a death penalty. If it turns out that Blacks have a substantially greater chance than Whites of actually being sentenced to death for the very same kinds of crimes for which judges or juries have discretionary powers to either sentence to death or prison, then I think we're definitely looking at a problem of discrimination at some level.

S: I'm trying to find that. . . . There's a lot here, and as I've said, none of it is properly organized yet.

P: But I would still say that even in that case we would need to look behind the statistics in order to discover exactly why the discrimination is taking place and at what precise juncture within the judicial process it occurs. If we are going to make meaningful efforts to root out the problem, then we need more information. We have to know what the problem is and discover its real cause. Statistics of the sort we've been considering can only point toward the difficulty without fully identifying it. They can only tell us that there really is a problem if we have the right sorts of statistical data and we interpret them carefully and correctly. After we have rightly inferred that they point toward a problem, then we still have to look beyond the statistics to uncover the real cause so that we can set about trying to correct it and make things better for everyone.

C: I agree with that.

S: Who doesn't?

P: Regrettably, there are persons in every society who fear and hate whatever is different from themselves. When those kinds of prejudices are institutional, when they dictate how the basic structures of law and government function, as they definitely have to a greater or lesser extent in many periods of American history and certainly in other cultures as well, then justice itself requires a fair and equitable impartial administration of the law in order to correct the imbalance. I was discussing this with C in connection with the image of justice personified holding a scale in which to weigh evidence and apportion punishments appropriately to offenses but also as being blindfolded. I take that to mean that when justice is properly managed it needs to be blind, indifferent, to a person's gender, race, religion, economic status, and so on, especially when an individual has been accused of a crime and is at risk of suffering some kind of punishment, whether it's a fine, imprisonment, the death sentence, or any other penalty.

C: Do you also agree that in the past most definitely and probably to a large extent even today racial minorities in the United States have suffered unfair treatment at the hands of the judicial system? I think that this Death Penalty Focus organization that S has found out about understands this exactly right and uses these facts recorded in their statistics to argue that capital punishment is inherently discriminatory to Blacks. If that's true, then that's a very good reason for abolishing the death penalty.

P: If, if, if. Yes, if all those ifs are true, then maybe there's an argument for rectifying the criminal justice system, including administration of the death penalty. What I don't agree is, first of all, that the statistics we've seen so far warrant the conclusion that the death penalty even as it's currently practiced needs to be abolished.

Look, we'd also be wrong as a society to be unfairly sentencing any sociologically identifiable group to prison terms on the basis of race or gender or religion or sexual orientation. That's just plain wrong. Justice must never peek beneath the blindfold to see who's Black and who's White, who's Christian, Jewish, or Muslim, who's male and who's female, and so on, especially when it comes to sentencing persons convicted of a crime, but in fact at absolutely every stage of the judicial process. It's not *justice* in the true sense of the word if it's *pre*judicial in any way or if it doesn't depend simply on the best determination of the facts about an individual's behavior as to whether that person has violated the law. Now, I think that anecdotally we could also probably agree that Blacks in the United States have been unfairly subject to incarceration under the law.

Probably, although S hasn't as yet produced any statistics on these matters, Blacks more often than Whites are sentenced to prison terms for committing the same crimes, and probably they are more often charged, tried, and convicted for doing the same things in breaking the same laws than Whites. That's completely unacceptable. But you're not arguing that therefore we ought to eliminate prison terms for everyone, are you? I thought your position was that we ought to enforce life sentences without the possibility for parole. If your reasoning is that we ought to abolish the death penalty because it's unfair to Blacks, then in all consistency you ought to argue that we also ought to abolish the prison system altogether for the same reason, proceeding anecdotally here again because, or let's say if, it's also unfair to Blacks.

C: No, that's not what I'm saying.

P: I realize that's not what you're saying. But it looks to me as though that's what you must be committed to believing, whether you're aware of it or not, and whether you happen to say it or not. Of course that's too extreme. If we abandon judicial punishment altogether just because it's been racially prejudicial, unfair to certain sociological groups, then we give up on any possibility of enforcing the law. And you know where that leads in next to no time at all—to the complete breakdown of society and degeneration into social chaos and lawlessness.

C: You're right that I want to preserve the prison system and especially lifetime imprisonment without the possibility of parole as a more humane alternative to the death penalty.

P: Well, I don't think you can have it both ways. If your argument is that the death penalty should be abolished because it's unfair to racial minorities in our society and if the prison system generally is also unfair in just the same way to the same racial minorities, then I think the conclusion on that way of reasoning is inescapable that the prison system generally should also be abolished.

C: I don't want that.

P: No. I don't think any of us thinking rationally would. What we need to do, I believe, is to reform the judicial system generally so that no one is treated unfairly at any stage of the process, including any aspect of law enforcement and any component especially of investigation, prosecution, sentencing, or punishment. Now, if the right conclusion is that we need to fix the administration of justice so that it's fair to everyone regardless of who they are, then that leaves the whole question of the morality of the death penalty in particular completely untouched. Probably, anecdotally, you're right that the death penalty has been unfair to Blacks in the United States. We should all hope and we should all work toward the day when that is no longer the case. By itself, however, that doesn't mean that we should do away with the death penalty. It's not a good enough reason, other things being equal, for abolishing capital punishment. At most this anecdotal evidence, to whatever extent it can be backed up with good scientific data and properly interpreted statistical analysis, argues for correcting the justice system generally, including the administration of the death penalty. It's not a reason to outlaw capital punishment altogether.

S: You've convinced me.

C: What? That the death penalty should stay?

P: I haven't tried just now to prove that. I'm only saying that the fact, if it is a fact, that racial minorities are treated unfairly in being sentenced to death for crimes in disproportionate numbers compared to other sociological groups, then that fact alone doesn't logically imply that we should therefore abolish the death penalty on the grounds that it is racially discriminatory. I agree, of course, that the system probably has been and to a large extent still is racially discriminatory. I agree that that's a very bad thing. I agree that we are morally obligated to do something about it. But I don't agree that what we are morally obligated to do about it is to abolish the death penalty.

C: You want us to reform the judicial system generally so that there's no racial discrimination in it anywhere.

P: Yes, of course. Absolutely. And not just racial discrimination, but I think that any kind of unfairness or discrimination is morally wrong and should be eliminated from the justice system wherever it exists. There is no justice where there is unfairness; justice means fairness in the sense of impartiality and in the proper allocation of punishments to crimes.

S: That's surely right.

P: What we can say more positively about the justice system even in its current state is that the use of DNA evidence to exonerate prisoners who have been wrongly convicted, whether or not they're on death row, has been effectively used to free both Blacks and Whites when there is scientific confirmation of their innocence. This process goes on in other ways too, although proof by DNA is particularly dramatic since the science is relatively new and generally considered conclusive. From what I can see when I watch the news, however, is that there doesn't seem to be any concerted effort within the justice system to use DNA evidence only to free Whites and not to free Blacks. I've seen many recent cases of Blacks and Whites being released from prison, even after years of wrongful conviction, when there is good evidence in support of their innocence. That's a good and hopeful sign as far as I'm concerned. In the future, perhaps there will be fewer and fewer mistaken convictions for crimes cutting across all racial and other sociological distinctions, thanks to modern forensic science.

C: I share your optimism.

P: Cautious optimism. There's a mountain of work to do before injustices against minorities in the United States and elsewhere in the world can be righted and before the long history of prejudice can be healed.

S: What I would add is that I think African Americans also want to have social policy concerning their immediate interests as members of a racial minority based on good hard scientific statistical evidence. Like everyone, they value the truth and need to have the law based on the real facts rather than impressions of what's true. How do you put it? Not on conjecture and anecdote.

P: Thanks. Yes, that's right. And while we're at it, let's take note of the fact that African Americans like every other group within society are often the victims of violent crime. Justice is also served by bringing the perpetrators of serious offenses against Blacks to trial. In some instances, where the best determination of the facts, appropriate application of the law, and all the relevant circumstances warrant it, criminals who have killed, abducted, or in other ways subject to capital statutes injured Black people, should equally be executed for their crimes. It doesn't matter whether the victims of crime or the criminals themselves are Black, White, or members of any other sociological group. What matters is that justice prevail. The death penalty for such crimes, including hate crimes, serves the interests of justice for Black people as much as it violates their rights when the death penalty is improperly, prejudicially, and to that degree unjustly administered.

C: You're not arguing that the death penalty should be preserved despite the fact that many Blacks have suffered from abuse of capital punishment laws just because some Blacks might take comfort in the possibility that the death penalty might also protect them, are you?

P: Not exactly. What I think justifies capital punishment is the argument that justice demands that persons who demonstrate by their actions a lack of respect for the moral right to life of others should themselves be required to forfeit their own lives when they are properly arrested, tried, convicted, and sentenced and, finally, when they have exhausted all avenues of legal appeal in trying to have the decision reviewed. I think that many African Americans as well as many White Americans, along with all other social groups and subgroups, are likely to appreciate the fact that a properly administered death penalty safeguards our shared way of life by upholding a standard of justice for the worst kinds of crimes of which any person of any color, gender, religion, sexual orientation, and so on might at any point be a victim.

C: Talk about anecdotal evidence.

P: Touché. Anyway, I'm not trying to say that the death penalty is morally justified because people want it or feel a sense of psychological closure or satisfaction when a capital offender pays for the crime by being executed. My arguments are meant to appeal to reason, not emotion. And, of course, I recognize that many people who have been victimized by capital crimes, if not in their own persons, then in those of their families and loved ones, want nothing whatsoever to do with the death penalty, that they object to it and reject it on ethical grounds of their own, much like C. "Don't kill for me" is the bumper sticker I've sometimes seen. Which I understand. Decent people want to be as conscience free as possible, and they may consider the death penalty to be a kind of moral taint. Nevertheless, I would say that what people want or don't want, what they are pleased or displeased by, their sense of satisfaction, closure, or irresolution when a criminal by whose actions they have somehow been affected has been executed or merely sentenced to a long or even a lifetime prison term, is entirely irrelevant to my argument in support of the death penalty. I'm arguing that capital punishment is not only morally permissible but morally obligatory by virtue of the objective requirements of justice. We must keep the balance pans of the scales of justice in equilibrium as much as possible, to the best of our abilities in the world of practical affairs. And I say again that I mean blindfolded justice, with no prejudices or sociological biases. That's what justifies the death penalty in my view, not the psychological effect on any particular segment of a society of having or not having a death penalty.

C: S, have you found what you're looking for yet?

S: Not so far. Look at this stuff. I've got two briefcases and a day pack full of papers, and nothing's really organized. Like I said, that's what I brought it along for, to work on this weekend. I'll let you know when I find something relevant.

C: Hey, pop the top and pass the caffeine.

P: My point is that I think that positive and negative reactions to the death penalty within the criminal justice system are mixed and divided in a way that cuts across all racial, gender and religious lines, as they do with respect to other kinds of divisions within society. I think that's pretty much what we ought to expect.

The general implication is that, even if one social group has been discriminated against by a social policy like the death penalty, we shouldn't presuppose that all members of that social group will necessarily be opposed to that policy. People think for themselves and are perfectly capable of weighing the evidence and arguments by their own lights, in deciding whether to support this or that course of action, whether it's really in or opposed to their ultimate long-term interests. And people will tend to disagree.

I guess I'm trying to say that even if Blacks have been discriminated against especially historically by the administration of the death penalty in this country and still today, that's no reason in and of itself to suppose that all Blacks are therefore opposed to the death penalty. Many of them will understand the value of upholding the requirements of justice by preserving capital punishment. Of course, no one will choose to be inherently disadvantaged by the system. No self-respecting person would tolerate that. Still, I believe, and I think that many persons from all cross sections of society are likely to agree with me, that certain kinds of crimes merit the death penalty, that the persons who commit those kinds of crimes deserve to die for what they have done, if they have been properly tried and convicted. I think that no other punishment is sufficient to serve the interests of justice. No other penalty is enough to pay for the deliberate cold-blooded premeditated murder of another human being.

C: Watch the road.

S: Here's something. This comes from Amnesty International. They're involved worldwide in efforts to promote human rights. One of their main concerns is to eliminate the death penalty. Here's part of what they write. This is from their website, http://www.amnesty.org/en/death-penalty. They start out with a general statement of position that reads, "The death penalty violates the right to life. It is the ultimate cruel, inhuman and degrading punishment. It has no place in a modern criminal justice system."

P: That's what they believe, but it's not an argument. They present it as though it were a fact that couldn't be reasonably disputed and with which everybody is sure to agree. It sounds rather dogmatic to me.

C: I respect the work that Amnesty International does.

P: Oh, so do I. They're an important force for bringing about respect for moral rights all around the world.

S: It says here that Amnesty International is "a founding member of the World Coalition Against the Death Penalty (WCADP)—a coalition of more than 40 human rights organizations, bar associations, trade unions and local and regional authorities, who have joined together in an effort to rid the world of capital punishment. Amnesty International coordinates the Anti-Death Penalty Asia Network (ADPAN). This was established in 2006 and is made up of lawyers, parliamentarians and activists from numerous countries including Australia, Hong Kong, India, Indonesia, Japan, South Korea, Malaysia, Mongolia, Pakistan, Papua New Guinea, Singapore, Taiwan and Thailand."

C: Impressive.

S: Hang on. They've got a lot more to say. Here's the first of several arguments. They write, "An execution, just like torture, involves a deliberate assault on a prisoner. Even so-called 'humane' methods such as lethal injection can entail excruciating suffering."

C: Exactly what I've been saying. So they do have an argument and probably more than one.

S: Oh, there's quite a bit here.

C: So, they're saying first of all that the death penalty is inhumane because it involves "excruciating suffering." If it were only suffering, I suppose that wouldn't be very convincing because even imprisonment involves suffering. If Buddhists are right, then to live is to suffer. That's the first of the Three Noble Truths of Buddhism. Excruciating suffering is something else.

P: Again, I'd say that if that were true, then there'd be no hope for euthanasia either. Surely with all our technology and knowledge of medicine we can put a human being to death painlessly. There can be mistakes made, obviously. I'm entirely opposed to any method of execution that causes undue pain. If lethal injection or something like it can be made virtually foolproof, then I think this first Amnesty International objection can be adequately answered.

Anyway, the mere fact that things *can* go wrong and that a condemned person *can* suffer even "excruciating suffering" can't possibly be a sound argument against implementing the death penalty because the same is true of medical procedures and many other practices. I don't think Amnesty International would want to abolish them just because they *can* cause excruciating suffering. You *fix* a procedure that has unwanted problems when there's a justification for using it; you don't simply abolish the procedure. Look, if capital punishment could be practiced only in a way that caused excruciating suffering or if the point and purpose of the death penalty were to cause excruciating suffering to a prisoner, then I think I would agree at once that it ought to be rejected as inherently inhumane. That would be torturing someone to death, which of course I could never support. But that's not the case, and accidents with modern methods of capital punishment are vastly in the exception rather than the rule.

S: I've got a file on that very problem. Here are some facts. In Lucasville, Ohio, on May 25, 2007, a man sentenced to death, Christopher Newton, took two hours to die by lethal injection. I've got a news release from the Associated Press. Apparently the condemned man was seriously overweight, 265 pounds, and the executioner couldn't find suitable veins on the man's arms to inject the chemicals. It says the procedure usually takes about twenty minutes when things go as they're supposed to. It seems there was another case in Ohio about a year earlier, involving a man named Joseph Lewis Clark. He was a longtime intravenous drug user, and again the executioner couldn't find a vein for the needle.

P: That's objectionable in both cases, of course. But it sounds like the problem was the mental anxiety involved in the delay. Do your articles say anything about the prisoners experiencing "excruciating suffering"?

S: No. Actually, the article says, "But Newton, who had insisted on the death penalty as punishment and made no attempt to appeal, chatted and laughed with prison staff throughout the delay. It took so long that the staff paused to allow Newton a bathroom break."

P: I rest my case.

S: There's more. It says here, "Gov. Ted Strickland, a Democrat who took office in January, said every precaution was taken to make sure Newton was treated respectfully and was not in pain. He said he understood why death penalty opponents wanted a moratorium, but 'I think what happened today is not any supporting justification for that.'"

P: That seems right. And that's fully in accord with my sense of how the death penalty should be humanely administered. There might be difficulties and delays in using the method if it's hard to find a vein on a particular prisoner for one reason or another. But that would also be true if the person was a patient in the hospital being prepped for surgery and the anesthesiologist couldn't find a good vein. Would Amnesty International or other opponents of the death penalty recommend abolishing surgery and other medical procedures involving intravenous injections just because of the condition of some people's veins? What did this guy Christopher Newton do, anyway? Why was he sentenced to death?

S: It says here, "He was put to death for beating and choking cell mate Jason Brewer, 27, in 2001 after they argued during a chess game. He had slammed Brewer's head onto the floor, stomped his throat and cut a piece from his orange prison suit to strangle him."

C: But did Newton actually kill Brewer?

S: I don't know. It doesn't say. It seems like it. The article says that a letter Newton wrote was read after his execution apologizing to Brewer's family.

P: Anyway, the delay doesn't seem to have actually caused the executed man any suffering, at least in this case. The chemicals used in lethal injection are generally effective. It's possible that the persons who administer this method of execution need better training. I would support that if it turned out to be true.

S: The article adds, "Problems with injection executions have caused delays in other states, including one in Florida last December that prompted Gov. Jeb Bush to suspend executions as a commission examines its procedures." I've got the report for that case too. It's also from the Associated Press, December 14, 2006. This was in Starke, Florida, and the executed man was Angel Nieves Diaz, who was fifty-six. He was convicted for murdering a topless bar manager twenty-seven years before. Diaz took thirty-four minutes to die and "appeared to grimace before dying." Apparently Diaz needed two doses of lethal chemicals because he had advanced liver disease. It's the liver that has to metabolize the poison used in execution by lethal injection, so I guess if it's diseased, then an unusual amount of the chemicals is needed.

P: Interesting. But the only evidence that Diaz suffered was that he "appeared to grimace"? I wonder how often that isn't true of persons receiving anesthesia? Heck, I grimace and sometimes holler a little when I'm getting a flu shot or donating blood. I don't like needles. I think a lot of people don't. It might also have been a purely physiological reaction to the procedure that didn't indicate anything about his state of mind. That by itself doesn't make execution by lethal injection inherently cruel or excessively traumatic. I don't think by itself it qualifies as causing the executed person "excruciating suffering" in Amnesty International's terms. Does Amnesty International have anything more to back up their claim that execution by lethal injection causes excruciating suffering in any instances at all?

S: There's nothing here about that. Maybe they've got other information somewhere else. I can look around. What it does say in this Associated Press article about Diaz is that, "moments before his execution, Diaz again denied killing Joseph Nagy during a robbery at the Velvet Swing Lounge. There were no eyewitnesses to Nagy's December 29, 1979, murder. Most of the club's employees and patrons were locked in a restroom, but Diaz's girlfriend told police he was involved."

P: Now, that's different. If there were questions about his guilt or innocence, then there's another argument as to whether he should have been convicted and therefore as to whether he should have been executed.

C: But that's always a possibility when a death sentence is issued. We can never know for sure whether a condemned person is really guilty and whether the person deserves capital punishment.

P: I think there are degrees of doubt. We don't have all the evidence that the judge and jury must have seen and heard. I can't imagine that Diaz was sentenced to death merely on the statement of his girlfriend, as the article seems to imply.

S: Another aspect of the case is that Diaz was a native of Puerto Rico, which abolished the death penalty already in 1929. The governor of Puerto Rico sought clemency for Diaz but was denied. Anyway, the article also cites a Florida Department of Corrections spokeswoman named Gretl Plessinger, who, quote, "said she doesn't believe Diaz felt any pain and had liver disease, which required the second dose." The prison system in Florida and the governor's office does not consider the Diaz case to represent a botched execution. Still, Florida decided as a result to suspend executions temporarily until a commission could study the incident and decide whether any revisions of the execution protocol should be made.

P: That seems entirely appropriate to me. If they've encountered technical or training problems, they should do whatever it takes to make the method as expeditious and painless as possible. But it is after all a punishment. And it sounds like Newton, unlike Diaz, acknowledged his guilt and admitted the justice of his being sentenced to death.

C: Just because he accepted the sentence and wanted to die doesn't mean he thought it was an act of justice for him to be sentenced to death. Maybe he simply didn't want to spend the rest of his life in jail. I think a certain number of inmates prefer death to life in prison. They are being punished for terrible crimes, after all, so we shouldn't necessarily give them what they want. As for Diaz, what if he wasn't really guilty? What if he didn't really kill the club owner and was sentenced to death and executed for a crime he didn't commit?

P: The mere fact that he denied murdering the club owner doesn't mean he didn't do it. Lots of criminals refuse to admit their guilt; many of them don't want to acknowledge what they've done even to themselves. They try to manipulate other people's opinions of them, and many times they don't want people to think they've committed such a terrible crime even as they're about to pay for what they've done.

C: Yes. But, still, he might have been innocent . . .

S: There's more on this. In the United States in 2007, executions dropped to a thirteen-year low. Only forty-two people were put to death in the United States in 2007, which is down 57 percent from 1999, when ninety-eight death row inmates were executed.

C: Where is that information coming from?

S: It's a report by the Death Penalty Information Center, which is a Washington, D.C.–based public interest group that opposes capital punishment. The report is quoted in a transcript from CNN in Washington, dated December 18, 2007. It's a news analysis in connection with two events. New Jersey banned executions in December 2007, when the U.S. Supreme Court had imposed a moratorium on execution by lethal injection until it could determine whether the three-chemical mixture used in the procedure constitutes cruel and unusual punishment. Now, get this, it says here, "since [lethal injection] may cause excruciating pain to inmates unable to express discomfort."

C: That's almost exactly the wording in the Amnesty International document.

P: If it's true that the method is all that painful, then I agree it should be reviewed and replaced with something more humane.

C: And if there's nothing that works painlessly?

P: I can't believe that there's not a way to put people painlessly to death. They knock patients out with anesthesia for painful operations all the time, and the patients never feel a thing. There must be a way to do that for persons who have been sentenced to execution. If the current method doesn't kill painlessly, then another method should be found.

S: Some of this CNN report supports C's position. Wait, though, here's something P will be interested to hear. The report quotes somebody named Kent S. Schneidegger from the Sacramento-based Criminal Justice Legal Foundation. He says, "I think the main problem is that the death penalty is not being imposed enough in . . . urban jurisdictions . . . I think people of the cities are not getting the quality of justice that people elsewhere receive. I think we need to build support for the death penalty and need to impose it more regularly where it is warranted."

P: So, professional and legal opinion is divided on the capital punishment question.

S: That's the picture here. The CNN report continues, "New Jersey's legislature voted last week to outlaw the death penalty—the first state to do so in 42 years—and Gov. Jon Corzine signed the measure into law Monday. At the same time, he commuted the sentences of the eight men on the state's death row. The move was largely symbolic, since no executions have occurred there since 1963."

C: Bravo.

S: But the report also says, "Similar bills in Nebraska, New Mexico and Montana have failed this year in the legislature. State lawmakers in Maryland, Colorado, North Carolina, Tennessee and California are also considering abolishing the death penalty, but no bills have been introduced."

P: The question C and I have been considering is whether the death penalty *should* be abolished. If these states follow New Jersey's recent lead or if the Supreme Court declares capital punishment to be unconstitutional, then our issue becomes whether they were right to do so, whether they should have abolished capital punishment, or whether they have acted against the real interests of justice by doing so.

S: Are you talking about *Baze v. Rees*? That was the case in Kentucky that the U.S. Supreme Court recently heard.

P: How recently?

S: I've got the documents right here. Hmm. . . . It looks like the case was argued before the Court on January 7, 2008, and decided April 16, 2008. That's just two days ago. The ruling is numbered 07-5439.

C: And the decision was?

S: The Court upheld the constitutionality of lethal injection as a method of execution that does not violate the Eighth Amendment to the U.S. Constitution prohibiting cruel and unusual punishment. The decision had direct application to the state of Kentucky, where the suit originated, but it has implications for all thirty-six U.S. states that use lethal injection and the federal government, which also executes criminals by lethal injection. Of the thirty-six states that execute criminals by lethal injection, thirty of them use the same standard combination of three drugs that Kentucky has as part of its execution protocol.

C: Well, I'm enormously disappointed. How could the Court have made that ruling?

S: The case came about because convicted murderers who were sentenced to death in Kentucky state court filed suit with the Supreme Court alleging that lethal injection violated the U.S. Constitution ban on cruel and unusual punishment. The state trial court held extensive hearings and concluded that the method of execution was in principle humane and that there was negligible risk of its being improperly administered, thus upholding its constitutionality. The Kentucky Supreme Court agreed, maintaining that the three-drug method does not violate the Eighth Amendment because it does not create a substantial risk of wanton and unnecessary infliction of pain, torture, or lingering death.

C: I guess that's what we might expect.

P: So, then the case went to the Supreme Court?

S: Right. The petitioners took their case there and the Court decided to hear the arguments. The decision was written by Chief Justice John Roberts, joined by Justice Anthony Kennedy and Justice Samuel Alito. Here's what they wrote in their Judgment, 217 S.W. 3d 207, affirmed—in case you ever want to look it up. They say, and I'm just quoting some of the highlights, "To constitute cruel and unusual punishment, an execution method must present a 'substantial' or 'objectively intolerable' risk of serious harm. A State's refusal to adopt proffered alternative procedures may violate the Eighth Amendment only where the alternative procedure is feasible, readily implemented, and in fact significantly reduces a substantial risk of severe pain."

C: What about all those reports of things going wrong in Ohio and elsewhere?

P: Apparently the Court took all of those reported facts and findings into consideration in applying legal precedent to their interpretation of the Constitution.

S: That seems right. Here's how the report continues. They say, "This Court has upheld capital punishment as constitutional." They refer, let's see, to *Gregg v. Georgia*, 428 U.S. 153. Then they write, "Because some risk of pain is inherent in even the most humane execution method, if only from the prospect of error in following the required procedure, the Constitution does not demand the avoidance of all risk of pain. Petitioners contend that the Eighth Amendment prohibits procedures that create an 'unnecessary risk' of pain, while Kentucky urges the Court to approve the 'substantial risk' test."

P: What's that?

S: Here's what they say:" "This Court has held that the Eighth Amendment forbids 'punishments of torture, . . . and all others in the same line of unnecessary cruelty,' *Wilkerson v. Utah*, 99 U.S. 130, such as disemboweling, beheading, quartering, dissecting, and burning alive, all of which share the deliberate infliction of pain for the sake of pain. . . . Observing also that '[p]unishments are cruel when they involve torture or a lingering death[,] . . . something inhuman and barbarous [and] . . . more than the mere extinguishment of life,' the Court has emphasized that an electrocution statute it was upholding 'was passed in the effort to devise a more humane method of reaching the result.'" They refer to a previous New York case of *Kemmler*, 136 U.S. 436.

C: Electrocution as a humane method of capital punishment? You have to wonder whether any of the Supreme Court justices have ever actually witnessed a convict being electrocuted.

P: Well, have you?

C: No, of course not.

S: Here's the part that's relevant to the new decision concerning the petition from the Kentucky death row inmates. The report states, "Although conceding that an execution under Kentucky's procedures would be humane and constitutional if performed properly, petitioners claim that there is a significant risk that the procedures will not be properly followed—particularly, that the sodium thiopental will not be properly administered to achieve its intended effect—resulting in severe pain when the other chemicals are administered. Subjecting individuals to a substantial risk of future harm can be cruel and unusual punishment if the conditions presenting the risk are 'sure or very likely to cause serious illness and needless suffering' and give rise to 'sufficiently imminent dangers.'" That precedent comes from *Helling v. McKinney*, 509 U.S. 25. Now they write, "To prevail, such a claim must present a 'substantial risk of serious harm,' an 'objectively intolerable risk of harm.' *Farmer v. Brennan*,

511 U.S. 825. . . . For example, the Court has held that an isolated mishap alone does not violate the Eighth Amendment, *Louisiana ex rel. Francis v. Resweber,* 329 U.S. 459, because such an event, while regrettable, does not suggest cruelty or a 'substantial risk of serious harm.'"

C: Okay. But hasn't that already been shown in all the instances where things have gone wrong?

S: The standard procedure from what I'm reading requires that if, "as determined by the warden and deputy, the prisoner is not unconscious within 60 seconds after the sodium thiopental's delivery, a new dose will be given at a secondary injection site before the second and third drugs are administered."

P: There, you see. They've got it built into the protocol not to proceed with the drugs that can cause pain along with death unless or until they're sure that the condemned person is actually fully anesthetized.

C: And if things go wrong even with the anesthetic?

P: It seems that as far as the Court is concerned, the point is that the procedure in and of itself isn't designed to produce a painful death. Just the opposite, in fact. It's intended in every way to make sure that capital punishment is administered in such a way that no pain whatsoever is experienced. The Court recognizes that highly regrettable mistakes can occur, but they see the possibility of error in implementing the method as a different issue from whether the method is inherently cruel and unusual. They don't seem to think it is, and I guess that I would have to agree. The Court doesn't believe that there's a "substantial risk" in following the method that any prisoner need ever experience any pain in being put to death by the three-drug protocol and that the possibility of exceptions in which mistakes are made resulting in prisoner discomfort or even intense pain doesn't render the method unconstitutional.

S: That's also my understanding of the Court's conclusions. Here's some more from the report: "Petitioners' primary contention is that the risks they have identified can be eliminated by adopting certain alternative procedures. Because allowing a condemned prisoner to challenge a State's execution method merely by showing a slightly or marginally safer alternative finds no support in this Court's cases, would embroil the courts in ongoing scientific controversies beyond their expertise, and would substantially intrude on the role of state legislatures in implementing execution procedures, petitioners' proposed 'unnecessary risk' standard is rejected in favor of Farmer's 'substantial risk of serious harm' test. To effectively address such a substantial risk, a proffered alternative procedure must be feasible, readily implemented, and in fact significantly reduce a substantial risk of severe pain. A State's refusal to adopt such an alternative in the face of these documented advantages, without a legitimate penological justification for its current execution method, can be viewed as 'cruel and unusual.'"

C: So, it sounds as though the Court has adopted the "substantial risk" over the "unnecessary risk" test in determining whether it would be unconstitutional to use the three-drug method as amounting to cruel and unusual punishment just because they're unable or unwilling to evaluate the scientific evidence.

P: Supreme Court members aren't supposed to be professional scientists. They have a specialized competence as interpreters of the law, and that's all. They would be acting irresponsibly if they tried to judge the scientific basis for alternative methods of anesthetizing prisoners to be executed where there's another legal basis for reaching their decision. That's what they've done here, and I think they're right.

C: But don't you see that the whole issue is whether there exists a more humane method of inducing an anesthetic state before administering the other drugs that actually kill? That is unavoidably a scientific question, and the Court seems to be shirking the main issue because they can't follow the technical details. How is that fair for the condemned?

S: Anyway, here's what they've ruled: "Petitioners have not carried their burden of showing that the risk of pain from maladministration of a concededly humane lethal injection protocol, and the failure to adopt untried and untested alternatives, constitute cruel and unusual punishment."

P: So, they didn't prove their case.

S: Seems not.

C: That still doesn't settle the moral issue of whether it's wrong to execute criminals even in the most humane way possible.

S: It appears that the Court did in fact consider quite a bit of scientific evidence on other matters related to the case. They write, "It is uncontested that failing a proper dose of sodium thiopental to render the prisoner unconscious, there is a substantial, constitutionally unacceptable risk of suffocation from the administration of pancuronium bromide and of pain from potassium chloride. It is, however, difficult to regard a practice as 'objectively intolerable' when it is in fact widely tolerated. Probative but not conclusive in this regard is the consensus among the Federal Government and the States that have adopted lethal injection and the specific three-drug combination Kentucky uses. . . . In light of the safeguards Kentucky's protocol puts in place, the risks of administering an inadequate sodium thiopental dose identified by petitioners are not so substantial or imminent as to amount to an Eighth Amendment violation."

P: This is exactly what I've been saying.

C: All I'm hearing is that it's okay to kill prisoners with the three-drug method because the three-drug method is being widely used to kill prisoners.

P: But the Court's not trying to judge the morality of the death penalty, only whether it amounts to unconstitutional cruel and unusual punishment. For that question, the issue of whether the procedure is widely followed—and hence not unusual—is obviously relevant.

S: A lot of the dispute seems to go back to the issue of whether the method itself might be inherently objectionable, as opposed to the potential for its faulty application. The Court adds, "The charge that Kentucky employs untrained personnel unqualified to calculate and mix an adequate dose was answered by the state trial court's finding, substantiated by expert testimony, that there would be minimal risk of improper mixing if the manufacturers' thiopental package insert instructions were followed. Likewise, the IV [intravenous] line problems alleged by petitioners do not establish a sufficiently substantial risk because IV team members must have at least one year of relevant professional experience, and the presence of the warden and deputy warden in the execution chamber allows them to watch for IV problems. If an insufficient dose is initially administered through the primary IV site, an additional dose can be given through the secondary site before the last two drugs are injected."

P: So, there are safeguards.

C: Not enough to avoid the problems that prisoners in other states have experienced.

S: Here's the main final thrust: "Nor does Kentucky's failure to adopt petitioners' proposed alternatives demonstrate that the state execution procedure is cruel and unusual. Kentucky's continued use of the three-drug protocol cannot be viewed as posing an 'objectively intolerable risk' when no other State has adopted the one-drug method and petitioners have proffered no study showing that it is an equally effective manner of imposing a death sentence. Petitioners contend that Kentucky should omit pancuronium bromide because it serves no therapeutic purpose while suppressing muscle movements that could reveal an inadequate administration of sodium thiopental. The state trial court specifically found that thiopental serves two purposes: (1) preventing involuntary convulsions or seizures during unconsciousness, thereby preserving the procedure's dignity, and (2) hastening death. Petitioners assert that their barbiturate-only protocol is used routinely by veterinarians for putting animals to sleep and that 23 States bar veterinarians from using a neuromuscular paralytic agent like pancuronium bromide. These arguments overlook the States' legitimate interest in providing for a quick, certain death, and in any event, veterinary practice for animals is not an appropriate guide for humane practices for humans. Petitioners charge that Kentucky's protocol lacks a systematic mechanism, such as a Bispectral Index monitor, blood pressure cuff, or electrocardiogram, for monitoring the prisoner's 'anesthetic depth.' But expert testimony shows both that a proper thiopental dose obviates the concern that a prisoner will not be sufficiently sedated, and that each of the proposed alternatives presents its own concerns."

C: Am I getting this right? The Court decides that we shouldn't be as humane in executing criminals as veterinarians are in putting animals to sleep? And the argument is that what counts as humane for animals isn't a good guide to what counts as humane for humans? Shouldn't we be at least as humane in our treatment of human prisoners as we are of animals, as a kind of minimal benchmark?

P: Of course, but that's not the issue. I thought that the Kentucky petitioners were objecting to the administration of the second drug in the three-drug protocol because by paralyzing the muscles, it prevents prisoners being executed from revealing by body movement that the anesthetic hasn't really taken effect. Naturally, no humane death penalty advocate wants the condemned to suffer pain from the administration of the third drug, so the question is how to avoid situations where the anesthetic in the first drug doesn't work. The reasoning seems to be that if the anesthetic can result in inhumane, let's say, cruel and unusual, treatment of execution subjects and if failing to use anesthetic is also inhumane, then there simply is no humane method of execution. The judges disagreed. They argued on the basis of expert scientific medical testimony that a proper dose of the anesthetic is generally sufficient, so that maintaining muscle activity and mechanically monitoring the anesthetic's effectiveness are unnecessary. The fact that the three-drug method isn't used to put animals to sleep they deemed irrelevant not because they want to treat human prisoners less humanely than animals but rather just the opposite. The twofold purpose of the muscle suppressant in the second drug, they say, is to allow for a more quick and dignified death without muscle spasm. The same considerations don't apply to the cost-effective extermination of animals that, rightly or wrongly, are usually accorded less dignity in all aspects of life and death than human beings, so the fact that the second drug isn't used to kill animals has no relevance for the execution of human criminals.

C: You can put it that way if you like, but it sounds to me as though the second drug is used so that the witnesses to an execution can avoid seeing what really happens to a person when he or she is killed by being injected with poison. It's more neat and tidy and less burdensome to the memory and conscience of the executioner and whoever has to watch the prisoner die. If we actually saw how the third drug affects a human body strapped to a table, if we saw the convulsions and spasms, there'd probably be an immediate moratorium on all penal executions. As it is, the second drug just sanitizes an inherently inhumane procedure, for which all the talk about preserving the prisoner's dignity in death is nothing but hypocrisy. The second drug is just there to make it seem that everything is quiet and peaceful and nothing violent is being done when in fact the condemned's body would otherwise be wracked with brutal seizures and paroxysms.

P: And yet they don't feel a thing when the anesthetic in the first drug has been properly administered; they're already completely oblivious to anything that's happening, and they don't know what is or what would be taking place inside them. That's a lot more dignity and a lot more humanity than most of these capital offenders ever showed their victims. I honestly don't see any hypocrisy in this. We suppress muscle reaction in executing human criminals for the same reason that we don't abuse their bodies in other ways. The fact that a muscle suppressant is being used and the prisoners know that it is being used allows them also to accept their punishment as more dignified since they can know that they will simply be painlessly and peacefully put to sleep.

C: It all sounds a little too antiseptic to me. It's dishonest and concealing, covering up the awful truth about execution even when it's right in front of us. The problem is that once the second, muscle-paralyzing drug takes hold, those being executed have no way to signal anyone in case the first anesthetic drug was ineffective, leaving them to suffer all the painful effects of the third drug that actually kills them.

P: I suppose there are many ways to look at just about anything.

C: By the way, was the decision unanimous, or was the Court split?

S: It wasn't unanimous but by an overwhelming majority, seven to two. The judges affirming the constitutionality of capital punishment by lethal injection included Justices Roberts, Kennedy, Alito, John Paul Stevens, Antonin Scalia, Clarence Thomas, and Stephen Breyer, with only Ruth Bader Ginsburg and David Hackett Souter dissenting. Here's a representative summary of one of supporting opinions, written by Justice Breyer. I'm quoting: "Justice Breyer concluded that there cannot be found, either in the record or in the readily available literature, sufficient grounds to believe that Kentucky's lethal injection method creates a significant risk of unnecessary suffering. Although the death penalty has serious risks—e.g., that the wrong person may be executed, that unwarranted animus about the victims' race, for example, may play a role, and that those convicted will find themselves on death row for many years—the penalty's lawfulness is not before the Court. And petitioners' proof and evidence, while giving rise to legitimate concern, do not show that Kentucky's execution method amounts to 'cruel and unusual punishmen[t].'"

C: I predict that this controversy is just going to continue despite the Supreme Court's ruling, especially in connection with the second drug in the three-drug protocol.

S: Wait, here's another file. This should interest both of you. It's another CNN report. This time from April 30, 2007. The report quotes Dr. Jay Chapman, who is the inventor of the three-drug method of execution by lethal injection. Chapman's method was developed in 1977 and originally adopted by thirty-seven of the thirty-eight states that practice capital punishment. Now that New Jersey had discontinued using the method, there are only thirty-six. The report says, "But now, after concerns that instead of causing an instant death it sometimes provides a slow, painful one, Chapman has rethought whether his formula is optimal. They quote Chapman as saying, "'It may be time to change it,' Chapman said in a recent interview. 'There are many problems that can arise . . . given the concerns people are raising with the protocol it should be re-examined.'"

C: Who is Chapman?

S: Let me see. . . . Apparently he's a forensic pathologist, and he was chief medical examiner in Oklahoma and a longtime supporter of the death penalty. He designed the three-drug combination that has become the standard method of execution by lethal injection in the United States. First, there's an injection of anesthetic to render the condemned person unconscious, as we've said, then a paralytic agent to stop breathing, and finally a drug to stop the heart. The three-drug combination is sometimes called a "lethal cocktail."

C: That's grim.

P: I'm sure his intentions were good.

S: Back to the CNN report. It says, "A recent study found sometimes inmates given lethal injections slowly suffocate while conscious but unable to communicate. Judges have ruled the procedure unconstitutional in two states, and 11 states have stopped using lethal injection. One problem was illustrated last year when it took nearly 90 minutes to execute Joseph Clark, who'd murdered two people in Ohio. Witnesses reported that Clark raised his head off the gurney and said repeatedly, 'don't work, don't work,' and moaned and groaned as he struggled with prison officials. News accounts of the execution also quoted Clark as saying, 'Can you just give me something by mouth to end this?'"

P: Yikes. That's no good.

C: Terrible. This is what I'm talking about. This is what Amnesty International is talking about.

P: I agree, obviously. They should fix that. And they should indeed halt executions in the meantime until they arrive at a method that's truly painless. Even a convicted serial killer or terrorist shouldn't have to suffer that kind of death at the hands of the state. That's not the kind of death penalty I have in mind for criminals who I still think deserve to die for their crimes. I must say, though, that I just don't understand how the anesthetic doesn't work in these cases. How many surgeries are performed in the United States alone every day? Anesthetic seems to work okay in all those situations. Why can't they put someone out for a painless execution? Maybe the problem is they're using the wrong kind of anesthetic or they're relying on untrained or inadequately trained executioners on the prison staff. It's obviously a scientific, quasi-medical procedure. Maybe they should have only qualified professional anesthesiologists administering the anesthetic so that they can know with greater confidence that the prisoner is actually unconscious before they administer the other two drugs to stop the lungs and heart, or however the method is supposed to work.

C: If we didn't have a death penalty in the first place, we wouldn't have to worry about how to do it painlessly, and we wouldn't have these cases of persons who have suffered needlessly when they're being executed. Amnesty International is right. And even the inventor of lethal injection is saying it should be discontinued.

S: Reading further, it looks as though Chapman thinks the problem is with the second drug in the three-drug combination. That's the one that paralyzes the lungs. Chapman now says that he thinks the middle drug is unnecessary and is probably the cause of pain. There's also some indication that the anesthetic standardly used, sodium thiopental, doesn't completely anesthetize all persons.

P: So, that could be part of the solution. Eliminate the lung-paralyzing or asphyxiating drug and substitute a better anesthetic.

S: Chapman in the CNN report says, "He wouldn't change the third drug, potassium chloride, which is highly effective in stopping the heart and causing cardiac arrest." He's also got some ideas about why things have gone wrong in some of the executions. "Chapman still stands by his formula as a sound—if not perfect—method of execution. 'It works if it's administered competently,' he said. 'But you have to have some skills to do it. You have to have the ability to find a vein and mix the drugs, because [some of them] come as a powder.' He added"—I'm still quoting from the CNN news story—"He added that he's heard reports that in one execution, the IV needle was inserted incorrectly, pointing toward the prisoner's hand rather than his body. 'You have to be an idiot to do that,' said Chapman. . . . He also cited another 'incompetency': the execution of Angel Nieves Diaz last year that took 34 minutes because IV needles were inserted straight through his veins and into the flesh in his arms."

C: Well, if the method is so complicated and if there are so many possibilities for mistakes, then they should stop it altogether.

P: I would agree but only until they devise a better method.

S: Here's how the report ends. "Even proponents of the death penalty say they have doubts about whether the three-drug formula is the best way to execute someone. 'I think it's a dumb way to do it,' said Michael Rushford, president of the Criminal Justice Legal Foundation, a group that advocates the death penalty. 'It's a complicated procedure, and open to criticism.' Instead, Rushford said he supports using carbon monoxide, which he described as being 'simple, fast, and painless.'"

C: I would agree that if there are serious problems with lethal injection, then a more human method ought to be found. Still, nothing here changes my mind about whether the death penalty is required by justice in punishing certain kinds of crimes. I don't know whether carbon monoxide would be better. I guess some people choose that method to commit suicide, running their cars in a closed space. They'd have to redesign the cyanide gas chamber to make it work. Anyway, I'm not an expert on these things. They should find someone with the necessary qualifications who can prescribe a method of executing capital offenders that doesn't cause them any unnecessary pain.

S: Going back to 2006, here's a CNN report written by Bill Mears, titled "Justices Issue Key Death Penalty Rulings." I'm looking at a section of the article subtitled "Is injection method painful?" This is part of what it says, concerning a case the Supreme Court will hear concerning a man named Clarence Hill who's arguing that execution by lethal injection would constitute cruel and unusual punishment. The article reads, "Clarence Hill, who murdered a police officer, argued the drugs used could fail, leaving him conscious but paralyzed and unable to express his pain while strapped on a gurney. The state . . ."

C: What state?

S: Doesn't say. "The state claimed its execution methods have been used the same way many times previously, and that Hill raised his claims too late in the appeal process." Now get this. "The 48-year-old inmate had been scheduled to die January 25 [2006]. A lawyer accompanying him to the death chamber said Hill was strapped to a gurney with IV tubes attached, ready for the injection when [Supreme Court Justice Anthony] Kennedy issued a temporary delay. The specific legal questions dealt with whether Hill could make a last-minute claim on the method of execution, and whether he could properly claim a civil rights violation. Kennedy concluded he could. It means Hill's execution has been delayed indefinitely while he continues his appeals."

C: I hope they overturn his sentence.

S: I'm not sure that'll happen. I think at most they'll have to use a different method of execution. There are some other inmates who have expressed similar concerns and raised legal issues about the constitutionality of execution by lethal injection. Here's a stack of papers on Philip Workman, who's on death row in Tennessee. He was convicted of killing a policeman during a failed holdup at a Wendy's restaurant in 1981 when he was twenty-eight years old. He says that he'd prefer to die by electric chair because he's worried that he'll suffer a slow death and not be able to tell anyone what's happening.

P: What was the final outcome? Is he still on death row?

S: He was executed by lethal injection on May 9, 2007. So, I guess the temporary injunction, which was issued on May 4, held for only about six days.

C: It must be awful to have your hopes lifted for a reprieve and then have them dashed again.

P: What we see demonstrated over and over in these cases is that there is an active and meaningful appeal process. I think that no stone is left unturned in a sincere effort to make sure that only the guilty are executed and that the execution is done humanely.

S: Says here that Tennessee's execution instructions manual at the time of Workman's appeal was completely confused. Although the method of execution was supposed to be lethal injection, the manual required the inmate's head to be shaved and for officials to have a fire extinguisher ready, to prepare electrode gel, to have an emergency generator, and to have an electrician on hand. All of that would be needed for an execution by the electric chair but obviously not for execution by lethal injection. It seems to me that there must have been some serious incompetence in the process. Scanning down, I'm reading further below that the procedures manual for execution in Tennessee has now been rescinded and revised. The new manual apparently still calls for the original three-drug combination that other states have been using.

C: How can anyone call this kind of method humane? I think that execution, no matter how it's carried out, is inherently *in*humane.

S: Here's another argument from Amnesty International. Let's get back to them. They continue, "Capital punishment is irrevocable. All judicial systems make mistakes, and as long as the death penalty persists, innocent people will be executed."

C: Again, that's what I've been saying all along. I think this is the part of the death penalty that bothers me the most. I can imagine myself or someone I know being executed by mistake, even though they're completely innocent. That's a fate to be avoided at any cost. If you're imprisoned, you can always continue to hope that some day you'll be exonerated and set free.

P: Well, as you know, we've gone round on this argument quite a bit, and I don't have anything to add to what I've said before. I don't want any innocent person to be put to death, and I support any methods that minimize wrongful executions.

S: Amnesty International also describes the death penalty as "discriminatory and is often used disproportionately against the poor, the powerless and the marginalized, as well as against people whom repressive governments want to eliminate."

C: That's the problem. It has a potential for abuse built into it. If the death penalty were abolished, it couldn't be misapplied.

P: Outlawing the death penalty isn't going to stop tyrants or corrupt governments from harming people. They'll just find another way to eliminate their opponents. They don't need to do so under cover of the justice system in their countries. They operate in secrecy. We need to do whatever we can to protect those who are at the mercy of oppressive governments. If it helps the cause of freedom and human rights to pressure those governments to give up the death penalty, then I'm all for it. Remember, I'm not in favor of capital punishment everywhere and under all circumstances. I only want persons guilty of certain kinds of crimes to pay for their misdeeds with their own lives when to do so is required by the ideals of justice. I don't want innocent people to die, either at the hands of criminals or by criminal governments.

C: How in the world can we in the free world advocate against capital punishment if we continue to employ the death penalty here?

S: Good point, I think. Amnesty International, like the Death Penalty Focus group, also cites figures that show capital punishment doesn't provide a deterrent to violent crime. They write, "The death penalty does not deter crime more than other punishments. In Canada the homicide rate has fallen by 40 per cent since 1975; the death penalty was abolished for murder in 1976."

P: Problems with statistics again. There's a fallacy that logicians call *post hoc, propter hoc*. It means "After the fact, because of the fact." Just because something happens *after* something else it doesn't follow that it happens *because* of what occurred before. How do we know that the homicide rate in Canada wouldn't have dropped even if the death penalty were in place? How do we know that there wasn't a trend against homicide that had started for many years previously in Canada precisely because it had implemented a death penalty originally as a discouragement to violent crime?

C: Wouldn't that also be a *post hoc, propter hoc* argument?

P: I'm not making the argument. I'm just asking how can we know that that's not the case? Anyway, everyone knows that the homicide rate in Canada for a variety of reasons is extremely low. Why does Amnesty International refer to that case, which I think many criminologists would say is anomalous among contemporary societies. Don't they have any better, more representative statistics indicating that there's a positive correlation between homicides and the use of the death penalty or reduction in homicides and elimination of the death penalty? I think these kinds of statistics are inconclusive at best.

S: You might be interested in seeing this. The information comes from a website called Pro Death Penalty Webpage, and it's maintained by someone named Wesley Lowe. I found it at http://www.wesleylowe.com/cp.html. I can't decide how authoritative it is, some of it seems a little crankish. It's got a cartoon near the bottom of the page, for example, that shows an inmate being dragged off into the gas chamber by two prison guards followed by a priest or minister carrying a Bible, and the prisoner's saying, "But you can't do this. Life is sacred." And one of the guards answers, "Exactly." You can't imagine Amnesty International allowing that kind of thing in its brochures. I'll quote you some parts that I've printed out, and you can take it for whatever you think it's worth. On the topic of deterrence, the site has a crawl banner that reads, "Each execution deters an average of 18 murders according to a 2003 nationwide study. According to a 2006 study, the Illinois moratorium on executions in 2000 led to 150 additional homicides over four years following. From a 2004 study, every 2.75 years cut from time spent on death row, one murder would be prevented. In the US, during the temporary suspension on capital punishment from 1972–1976, the murder rate doubled."

C: What are these anonymous "studies" that are supposed to show all this?

P: They're no more anonymous than the ones that are cited to prove that the death penalty has no deterrent effect.

S: There is at least some information in the body of the website itself. Here's something of interest. "During the temporary suspension on capital punishment from 1972–1976," it says, "researchers gathered murder statistics across the country. In 1960, there were 56 executions in the USA and 9,140 murders. By 1964, when there were only 15 executions, the number of murders had risen to 9,250. In 1969, there were no executions and 14,590 murders, and 1975, after six more years without executions, 20,510 murders occurred rising to 23,040 in 1980 after only two executions since 1976. In summary, between 1965 and 1980, the number of annual murders in the United States skyrocketed from 9,960 to 23,040, a 131 percent increase. The murder rate—homicides per 100,000 persons—doubled from 5.1 to 10.2. So the number of murders grew as the number of executions shrank."

P: It makes sense to me that a potential premeditating killer would think twice before committing murder if he or she knew that the punishment might be his or her own death. Those figures must come from publicly available sources, so we could check on them in detail if we wanted.

S: Then the website quotes "Researcher Karl Spence of Texas A&M University." I'm not sure if that's the researcher who compiled the statistics I just quoted or a researcher who is interpreting the statistics or has an opinion about the death penalty. Anyway, the report as a whole is not as anonymous as the crawl. Spence is quoted as saying, "While some [death penalty] abolitionists try to face down the results of their disastrous experiment and still argue to the contrary, the . . . [data] concludes that a substantial deterrent effect has been observed . . . In six months, more Americans are murdered than have killed by execution in this entire century. . . Until we begin to fight crime in earnest [by using the death penalty], every person who dies at a criminal's hands is a victim of our inaction."

P: I don't regard any of this as conclusive. It's also just more *post hoc, propter hoc.* But I do think it helps to blunt the stock objections of death penalty opponents who frequently allege that capital punishment doesn't deter homicides and other violent crimes.

S: The site also refers to someone named Dudley Sharp of the criminal justice reform group Justice for All. Sharp is quoted as saying, "From 1995 to 2000, executions averaged 71 per year, a 21,000 percent increase over the 1966–1980 period. The murder rate dropped from a high of 10.2 (per 100,000) in 1980 to 5.7 in 1999—a 44 percent reduction. The murder rate is now at its lowest level since 1966."

C: I'd want to look very closely at those statistics, and I'd like to find out more about these so-called experts who are being quoted.

S: There's actually quite a few sources that take roughly this same point of view. Look at this file. It's as thick as the Los Angeles telephone book. And I've sampled only what's out there in print and electronic media.

C: For that matter, I'd like to investigate this website and see what kind of credentials the author has. This is contrary to everything I've seen in the anti-death-penalty literature. I thought it was well known that capital punishment is no deterrent to crime.

P: What would you expect? I'm suspicious too. But it does offer food for thought if respected researchers at universities and advocacy groups can offer statistics suggesting that the death penalty does in fact deter homicides. At least the correlation between implementation of the death penalty and a decrease in murders is significant; also, the increase in murders that seems to have accompanied moratoria on executions argues for some kind of cause and effect on criminal behavior.

C: It doesn't mean anything if statistics can be used to prove just the opposite conclusion too.

P: I don't know. I'd be the first to say that there are unlimitedly many other social factors that could be at work at the same time to account for these correlations. Still, it's interesting. And it makes sense to me. I never understood how eliminating the death penalty could so suddenly bring about a decrease in murders. What would be the causal mechanism at work? Are we supposed to believe that potential criminals are happier in a society that doesn't have the death penalty, so right away the next year they choose not to commit as many murders? I don't get it. And with actual names attached to the studies, we can look into the science behind the sociology and see whether we think there's anything of substance in these claims.

C: I just don't believe it. I don't think that criminals make those kinds of calculations about whether it would be worth it for them to kill somebody. They do it without thinking, or they do it assuming that they'll escape any kind of punishment at all, whether it's the death penalty or life in prison.

P: You seem to want to pick and choose the statistics that support what you already prefer to believe. That's not taking a scientific approach to public policy decision making.

C: Ditto.

S: Here's Amnesty International's final argument, at least in the source I've got handy here. They claim, "International human rights treaties prohibit courts sentencing anyone who was under 18 years old at the time of the crime to death, or executing them. But a small number of countries continue to execute child offenders, violating their obligations under international law."

P: I agree entirely that children should never be subject to the death penalty. When I say that I advocate capital punishment, I'm talking about mentally competent adults only. I'm all in favor of acting along with Amnesty International to prevent any governments from executing children under the age of eighteen. It's inexcusable. However, that fact doesn't detract in my opinion from the legitimacy of implementing the death penalty for special categories of crime under certain circumstances when committed by morally responsible adults.

C: I'm just worried that if we have the death penalty for any kind of crimes, the most serious homicides committed by morally responsible adults, then over time it can start to be applied to more and more kinds of categories. There is an excuse for using capital punishment on other persons than it was originally intended for.

P: Why would anything like that happen?

C: Bit by bit, the government could decide that persons aged seventeen should be tried as capital offenders and possibly sentenced to death. And once that was established, they could lower it again to sixteen and so on. Or they could extend the coverage of death penalty cases from homicide and terrorism to trying to undermine the government by expressing dissent or demonstrating against officials or policies.

P: There are safeguards against that kind of thing. What you're describing is sometimes known as a slippery slope argument. If we set a supposedly dangerous precedent, then we might continue incrementally moving in a direction that we would all finally find unacceptable. Give 'em an inch, and they'll take a mile.

C: That's right.

P: I think that's really a baseless fear. There are powerful safeguards on these matters if you're talking about the United States. It's no accident that the Supreme Court, as the highest court in the land, has ruled against death penalty sentencing for children under the age of eighteen. The Supreme Court can't be overturned in legal matters, unless special legislation or an executive order is passed, and there are numerous checks and balances also on that kind of maneuver.

C: At least we can agree on that.

P: Oh, I think we agree on lots of stuff. Where we disagree is significant, though. We disagree about how the perpetrators of the worst offenses in society should have to pay for their crimes.

C: Right. Because you think that people have to deserve the moral right to life by virtue of their actions, and I think that people have the moral right to life no matter what they do, just by virtue of being human.

P: Did you know that the U.S. Supreme Court in 1976 banned use of the death penalty for rape? I support that decision too, although I think that rape is a terrible crime and should be prosecuted to the fullest extent of the law. It fits my sense of the ideal of justice not to punish rape with the death penalty because, as awful a crime as rape is, it doesn't amount to the murder of an innocent human being. It's not on the same level. So the scales of justice in my metaphor are improperly tipped when a crime like rape is punished by death. The same is true, I believe, of sentencing children to death, even when they participate in the same kinds of crimes that I think should be treated as capital offenses when they're committed by morally responsible adults.

C: I guess that's reassuring.

P: The whole trend, at least in the United States, is against expanding the use of the death penalty except in the case of homicide and terrorism. So, if anything, the slippery slope is leading the other way, toward the gradual erosion of the use of capital punishment in judicial matters. It's not used in rape trials, not for children under eighteen. In my view, the proper emphasis is being given to the death penalty as a punishment exclusively for those crimes where it's strictly demanded by justice.

C: What about high treason, as in Great Britain? Can't you be sentenced to death in the United States for committing an act of high treason against the state?

P: Maybe. I don't know for sure.

C: If so, then I still think I have some concerns because the concept of treason is vague. I suppose it means acting against the security, safety, and military secrecy of the government. But that could be interpreted strictly or loosely, and, if loosely, it could include such things as voicing opposition to the government, expressing opposition or hostility toward persons in power, and other things besides.

P: That's always a concern. We have to rely on the free press and the history of respecting civil disobedience as bulwarks against incursions into our freedoms. If things get that desperate in a democratic society, I think that capital punishment will be the least of our concerns. Countries that still try to cloak their repression of citizens by wrongful use of the death penalty are under intense scrutiny from their own people and abroad by the international community. I think that these issues, other things being equal, are beyond the scope of the questions we've been considering about the morality of the death penalty in a free society.

C: I wish I could believe that . . .

S: Amnesty International then closes its information page with the following facts. I don't know how recent any of these data are, but here's what they say. They list out a number of bulleted items. I'm quoting here:

- 135 countries have abolished the death penalty in law or practice.
- 62 countries retain and use the death penalty, most often as a punishment for people convicted of murder.
- At least 1,591 people were known to be executed in 25 countries during 2006. The true figure was certainly higher.
- 91 per cent of all known executions in 2006 took place in China, Iran, Pakistan, Iraq, Sudan, and the USA.

C: Any reactions?

P: Well, I'm reassured that Amnesty International reports that most countries implement the death penalty for persons convicted of murder. That's just the kind of crime for which I think that capital punishment is appropriate. I also think the list of countries in which executions took place seems strange to me. I know that Japan and Turkey have capital punishment. I wouldn't be surprised if Japan didn't have many executions, so it's probably in the remaining 9 percent after you subtract the 91 percent of all known executions that Amnesty International refers to.

I don't know about Turkey. They might be working toward eliminating the death penalty entirely because they have aspirations of entering the European Union, and it's a charter requirement that you can't be part of the EU if you practice capital punishment. What about Saudi Arabia? Singapore? And the former Soviet Union? Even Great Britain, as we said, still has capital punishment on the books in cases of high treason. It's interesting that fully one-third of all countries have a death penalty. We can't say that it's a choice for the administration of justice that is somehow peculiar or unusual. Many countries choose not to execute their capital offenders, but it's not as though the United States is alone among nations in having a death penalty. We're not in the majority, but it's a rather substantial minority.

C: If you think it's a mark of distinction or of progressive law enforcement to be numbered among countries like Iraq, Iran, Sudan, Pakistan, and Saudi Arabia, then I think the United States is in rather serious moral trouble and in highly morally compromising company.

S: Here's another source. As to Saudi Arabia, it says the sheikdom executed thirty-nine people in 2006, twenty-six of whom were foreigners. In 2007, however, they had executed more than one hundred persons already in July.

P: I'm not surprised. I'm just as opposed to the barbaric amputation by sword of a thief's hands in Saudi Arabia. They practice a very literal interpretation of traditional Shari'a Islamic law. Countries like Iran that still use traditional methods of capital punishment like stoning to death, I think, should adopt more humane practices. Among other things, they stone women to death for adultery. The Saudis publicly behead capital offenders with a sword.

S: We'd better think about pulling in for gas. You haven't been paying attention to the fuel gauge, have you?

AFTERNOON INTERLUDE

C: P, you seem to think that the United States serves as a model of criminal justice for the rest of the world. But, you know, Europe is so much more advanced than the United States in having abolished the death penalty altogether.

P: Do you call that being advanced? It's advanced only if you accept any of the arguments against capital punishment. Those arguments don't look very strong to me.

S: I've got something here that might interest you both. It's an article by Charles Lane, who covers stories on the U.S. Supreme Court for the *Wash-*

ington Post. This is a photocopy of an article from the newspaper for June 4, 2005, page A17. It gives a different perspective on the death penalty question in Germany. I'll read the highlights. It says, and I quote, "In the debate between Europe and the United States over the death penalty, no country is more vocal than Germany. German media regularly decry executions in Texas. A recent U.S. Supreme Court case concerning the rights, under international law, of foreign defendants in capital cases grew in part out of a German lawsuit before the World Court on behalf of two German citizens on death row in Arizona. (The Supreme Court dismissed the case on May 23 for technical reasons.) German objections to capital punishment slowed Berlin's cooperation with the U.S. prosecution of alleged al Qaeda operative Zacarias Moussaoui, who faces the possibility of the death penalty—though the two countries eventually worked out an agreement."

P: I'm not surprised to see that a country's opposition to the death penalty is directly related to its political self-interest.

S: Wait, there's more. Let me finish. The article continues, "Contrasting their nation's policy with that of the Americans, Germans point proudly to Article 102 of their Basic Law, adopted in 1949. It reads, simply: 'The death penalty is abolished.' They often say that this 56-year-old provision shows how thoroughly the postwar Federal Republic has learned—and applied—the lessons of Nazi state-sponsored killing. (Communist East Germany kept the death penalty until 1987.) But the actual history of the German death penalty ban casts this claim in a different light. Article 102 was in fact the brainchild of a right-wing politician who sympathized with convicted Nazi war criminals—and sought to prevent their execution by British and American occupation authorities. Far from intending to repudiate the barbarism of Hitler, the author of Article 102 wanted to make a statement about the supposed excesses of Allied victors' justice."

C: That doesn't mean they weren't right to abolish the death penalty.

P: Maybe not. But I think it does call the moral motivations for the original elimination of the death penalty in Germany into serious question.

C: Anyway, Germany is just one country in Europe. Most of the rest of Europe was victimized by Nazi oppression. You can't say that they've done away with capital punishment for the same reason as the Germans in 1949.

S: One final note. Lane also says this: "Meanwhile, there was little opposition in West Germany to capital punishment for ordinary criminals. A poll by the Allensbach Institute in February 1949 showed that 77 percent of West Germany's population favored it."

C: Well, they were wrong to approve of it. And what about the costs, I mean, in terms of human life and the perception of the value of human life and human dignity within a society and throughout the world? Also, what about the sheer expense in terms of a society's resources when it implements the death penalty?

P: Remember that my reason for advocating the death penalty has to do with considerations of justice. So I'm completely unmoved by questions about the comparative costs of maintaining a capital punishment system as opposed to life imprisonment without possibility of parole. If I recall correctly, a study was done in New Jersey that showed it was much more expensive to be ready for executions and to support all the appeals involved in death penalty cases than it would be simply to imprison capital criminals for life. That's probably true. But I don't care. Justice demands the death penalty in certain kinds of cases under certain kinds of circumstances, and, whatever it costs, that's a price that we as a society concerned about fulfilling the requirements of justice must be prepared to pay. Heaven knows we spend a lot of money on less important things.

S: Alright. Here's something. I just saw the New Jersey study you mentioned. It's a New Jersey Policy Perspectives report. It concludes that New Jersey's death penalty has cost state taxpayers $253 million since 1983, an amount in excess of what it would have cost to implement a life sentence without possibility of parole instead of capital punishment. Here's part of what the report says: "From a strictly financial perspective, it is hard to reach a conclusion other than this: New Jersey taxpayers over the last 23 years have paid more than a quarter billion dollars on a capital punishment system that has executed no one."

P: That's a little odd, isn't it?

C: How so?

P: It sounds at the end as though the main disappointment is that the state devoted lots of funds to having a death penalty but never actually used it. I doubt they'd complain about the money spent on screening airports for terrorists carrying bombs if it turned out that they didn't happen to catch any violent extremists. They'd say it was worth the money for the sake of readiness and precaution. They might even say that spending the money was worth it because it might have prevented hijackings.

S: There's more . . .

P: I suppose opponents of the death penalty are embarrassed to make the argument against capital punishment solely on the basis of trying to save money by enforcing life sentences instead of execution. I have to say, that does strike me as rather unseemly. Who can put a price on what a just society ought to do in order to uphold what its values demand? I find that kind of reasoning somewhat reprehensible.

C: There are always practical limits to what even the best-intentioned society can and cannot do with finite resources and multiple problems to address.

P: Granted. But look at it this way. I'm sure that if it turned out to be more expensive to house capital criminals for life than to execute them, virtually no one would want to be associated with the argument that therefore we ought to sustain and implement the death penalty for the sake of saving money. Everyone would say that a public policy decision based on that kind of pecuniary motivation would be outrageous by virtue of cheapening the lives of prisoners weighed against a bottom-line dollar figure in the state's fiscal bookkeeping. If the argument itself were sound, then those who support it ought to be willing to let it cut either way, depending on which judicial practice actually turns out to save more money. Of course, they won't do that.

What's good for the goose is good for the gander, I say. So, if no one is prepared to argue that we ought to execute rather than imprison capital criminals for life if that turns out to be lighter on the taxpayers' wallets, then they ought to be prepared to accept the opposite conclusion if someone can work out a way to make it financially less expensive to sentence criminals to execution rather than to life sentences without the possibility of parole. To my way of thinking, the entire issue ought to be decided exclusively on the basis of what justice requires. It's a justice-related controversy, so the only factor that's truly relevant is whether justice requires the death penalty in at least some criminal sentencings.

If the answer is yes, then the cost shouldn't matter as a reason for implementing capital punishment of those kinds of crimes. If the answer is no, then equally the cost shouldn't matter as a reason for proscribing the death penalty. We should abolish it at once in that case even if it turns out to be enormously more expensive to imprison capital offenders for life compared to what it would cost the state to execute them.

C: Forget the costs argument. I still don't agree that justice demands that we execute what you're calling capital offense criminals.

P: Haven't we been all over this before?

C: It's not my fault you're obstinate. I feel a responsibility to stick with my side of the dispute until I can make you see things from a morally proper point of view.

P: Obstinate?

C: Hear me out. You've emphasized an image of Justice as the goddess or personification of a certain judicial ideal. We both agree that justice should be blind in the sense of impartiality. Now what about the scales that Justice holds? The balance pans. I've heard your interpretation, but I'd like to offer a somewhat different spin on the same attribute. Here's what I want to say about the scales of Justice.

S: I want to hear this too.

C: You say that justice demands that we approximate as closely as we can an absolute standard in which punishments constitute a matching of penalty to offense. And you want to say that the only way to pay for a crime like first-degree cold-blooded premeditated murder, among other very serious offenses, is for the killer to be killed, to lose his or her own life as a consequence of an act of murder by judicial execution.

S: That sounds a little like the Lord High Executioner in Gilbert and Sullivan's comic opera, *The Mikado*. What does he sing? Something like, "My object all sublime. I shall achieve in time. To let the punishment fit the crime; the punishment fit the crime."

C: Yeah. And then it goes, "And make each penitent, unwillingly represent, an innocent source of merriment, of innocent merriment."

P: It's funny in that context, sure. Not to make light of a serious issue. But I think that punishments *should* fit the crime. A proper sentencing should always exact a penalty from a wrongdoer that is in accord with the requirements of justice so that, opera buffa aside, the punishment fits the crime. Take a life, lose your own life. Steal a car, pay for it by compensating the owner with money and with jail time. Why should a law-abiding citizen who loses property to a thief suffer any deficit? What's the car owner done wrong? And by that principle, if you kill someone in cold blood, the only way you can pay society back for that kind of crime is to forfeit your own life.

C: Yeah. I've got it. I know what you're saying. You've done an excellent job of making the position crystal clear. But do you remember what I was saying yesterday about the problem of playing God? Trying to do what only the goddess Justice can truly do is playing God or playing goddess.

P: I thought we'd dispensed with that slogan . . .

C: There's more to be said about this, much more. A god or goddess is infallible, but we are not. A god or goddess is omniscient, has a perfect knowledge of the facts and circumstances surrounding all our actions. So, such a being can exactly balance the scales of justice by arriving at a sentence for a crime that exactly fits the magnitude of the crime committed. We, however, as finite fallible human beings can never know for sure that we have done the work of justice correctly. We can only try our best in the most sincere way, in the Lord High Executioner's phrase, to make the punishment fit the crime. If we were gods and goddesses like Justice, then we could reasonably put the ideal you're holding out into practice. But the fact is that we can't. We can never know for certain whether a person is guilty of a crime, and that means that we can never know for certain when we sentence a person to death for a crime that we have in fact brought the scales of justice into balance.

P: I don't see how any of this is supposed to be new. This is what I understood you to be saying all along.

C: No. It's quite different, because I'm giving special content to what I mean by what's objectionable about playing God in having the extraordinary presumption to sentence another human being to death on the basis of what we fallibly believe that person to have done.

P: It's presumptuous?

C: Absolutely. We do not have the moral right to presume that we can set the scales of justice in exact balance by sentencing a capital offender to death because we can never know beyond a shadow of a doubt that a person being prosecuted has actually committed a crime.

P: Then, why isn't it equally playing God to sentence a capital offender to life in prison without the possibility of parole? If you're right, then we can't know beyond a shadow of a doubt that a convicted felon has actually done the crime. So, why isn't it presumptuous to sentence the person to any sort of punishment short of the death penalty?

C: Because in that case we're not trying to set the scales of justice in exact balance. We're only trying to contain the offender so that the individual cannot continue to commit those kinds of crimes, to isolate the offender for the protection of society. It is a punishment, to be sure. But as long as we're not attempting to mete out perfect justice for what someone has done in breaking the law, then we're not presuming to do what only a perfect being like God or the goddess Justice could properly do. In that case, we're not playing God.

The point is not to sloganize about respecting our limitations as finite beings capable only of finite fallible knowledge and certainly not to get religious about our civic duties within the judicial system. The point is rather to recognize that we cannot responsibly live up to the ideal of rendering perfect justice—or anything even remotely resembling it—in the case of capital crimes. If we are going to sentence someone to death for willful violent behavior resulting in another person's death, then we can aspire to set the scales of justice in balance only if we know for certain that the person has committed the crime. And that, realistically but speaking fictionally, is something that only God or a divine being like the goddess Justice could possibly do. Since in practice we must fall short of that ideal, we should acknowledge our limitations by not overstepping the bounds of our best efforts to ascertain the facts in a criminal proceeding.

P: So, if I understand your position, you're saying that if we can't know with full certainty that we are living up to the ideal of justice, which you seem to admit is in fact the proper standard, then we should simply give up altogether and redefine the purpose of justice as something different. We cannot infallibly know that we have balanced the scales of justice, so we should reject the goal of trying to achieve justice and instead simply house criminals in prison indefinitely to make sure they don't hurt anyone else. Is that it?

C: I wouldn't put it quite that cynically.

P: What's cynical about it?

C: First, I don't acknowledge exactly balancing the scales of justice as the real practical ideal of justice for human beings. It's arguably an ideal for an ideal being, like the goddess of Justice, but not for us. And I don't say that we should simply give up on the ideal because we can't achieve it. I'm saying that it was never our ideal in the first place. It's a fiction, as I said yesterday. We have no obligation to try to live up to fictional standards. I wouldn't accuse you of failing to meet your desire to support charitable causes just because you can't support all charities equally or with all your resources while still fulfilling your other obligations.

P: But don't you think I would be a better person if I *tried* to meet that ideal, even if I understood all along that the ideal was practically unattainable? Don't we do this all the time? I'm a better swimmer for trying to meet an Olympic gold medalist's record, but I know realistically that I will never be able to do so. The effort and the orientation toward an ideal goal drives me to try to be better than I would otherwise try to be, and that in turn causes me actually to do better than I otherwise would.

C: The difference—and the difference here is huge—is that the ideal you're talking about in balancing the scales of justice by handing out death sentences for criminals affects the lives of persons who may turn out later to have been entirely innocent of the capital crimes for which they were convicted.

S: That's what I've been looking for. Here's some more data. Again, it's from Death Penalty Focus. They say this: "The wrongful execution of an innocent person is an injustice that can never be rectified. Since the reinstatement of the death penalty, 123 men and women have been released from Death Row nationally . . . some only minutes away from execution. Moreover, in the past two years evidence has come to light which indicates that four men may have been wrongfully EXECUTED in recent years for crimes they did not commit. This error rate is simply appalling, and completely unacceptable, when we are talking about life and death."

C: There, you see? That's exactly what I'm saying.

P: I absolutely agree that the error rate is appalling and unacceptable. It should never happen. We should take every precaution to make sure it doesn't occur. I would say the same, however, for medical misdiagnoses and malpractice, for faulty engineering that results in accidental death, for bad judgment on the battlefield, including death by friendly fire, so-called collateral damage, which is just a euphemism for killing innocent bystanders, incompetent military leadership resulting in unnecessary troop losses, excessive force by the police, and a host of other accidental mishaps and deliberate abuses. What I wouldn't say, however, is that the right conclusion from our being appalled and finding those outcomes unacceptable should therefore be to stop practicing medicine, give up structural civil engineering, and dismantle the military and police. Similarly, and for precisely the same reason, governed by precisely the same logic, I wouldn't say that we should therefore abolish the death penalty.

C: Why? What useful purpose does it serve?

P: Even if capital punishment served no useful purpose, and that's something I don't agree about at all, I repeat that the justification for the death penalty is that it serves an ideal of justice that brings us as close as possible to apportioning punishment to crime in the case of what I call capital offenses. I believe in ideals, and I believe in trying to approximate them as best as we can, even when they are not always fully realizable. I think that we become better individuals and improve society when we at least try to live up to a noble ideal.

C: How is executing an innocent person noble?

P: The ideal of justice is noble. Executing an innocent person, I've already acknowledged, is appalling and unacceptable. I also think it's noble to cure disease but not to prescribe the wrong medicine that kills a patient. I also think it's noble to defend our society from its external enemies but not to cause unnecessary loss of life to our own soldiers or friendly noncombatants. What I take away from these examples is that we must repair a practice to make it work properly rather than eliminate it if there's a good justification for the practice in the first place. What you want to conclude, apparently only in the case of capital punishment, is that therefore we ought to discontinue the practice.

C: That's because I don't share your sense that there is any positive practical benefit to be derived from continuing the death penalty.

P: Really? None whatever?

C: None. What does society gain by killing someone instead of punishing them with life in prison and no parole?

P: If I may, I see your alternative mode of punishment for capital offenders as a refusal to accept the moral responsibility we have to uphold the highest standards of justice. By sentencing a capital offender to life in prison with no possibility of parole, you are in effect removing them from the rest of society just as though they had been executed, but you avoid taking upon yourself the full psychological responsibility for delivering the death sentence that justice requires.

C: Standing up for another person's life is certainly not an evasion of moral responsibility. Especially not when you consider that for all we know in any individual case the accused and convicted might actually turn out to be innocent—or to have been innocent, if the information comes too late to save the condemned person's life after an execution has actually been carried out.

P: I think our obligation is to prevent miscarriages of justice, not to do away with what justice requires of us as its morally responsible agents.

C: And the benefits of actually executing a capital offender? What are those again?

P: Now, remember, I'm prepared to defend the death penalty on the grounds that it's required by our moral obligation to try to fulfill an ideal of justice even if it has no practical benefits at all. But I think that as a matter of fact there are a number of distinct and important benefits to society that accrue from judiciously instituting a death penalty for the worst sorts of crimes.

C: And those would be?

P: Prosecutors often use the threat of seeking the death penalty in particular cases as a plea-bargaining incentive. Persons accused of serious crimes frequently have either committed other crimes themselves or know of other persons who have committed crimes. If they know the evidence is strong against them, then they understand, or their court-appointed lawyers quickly help them to understand, that they are probably going to prison for a long time, possibly for the rest of their lives. So, what do they have to lose? There's no motivation for them to cooperate with the authorities by telling what they know. If they want to save their lives, however, then in many instances, they might decide to reveal valuable information to the police that can help solve and prevent crimes, even save the lives of other innocent persons, in order to avoid having the prosecution seek the death penalty. If you take away the death penalty by abolishing capital punishment, then you also take away an extremely useful tool used by law enforcement and the judicial system.

S: I've heard about that. I think you're right that criminal prosecutors appreciate having the leverage that the threat of a death sentence affords in investigating crimes. They want to be able to close open-ended cases by discovering who might have committed particular crimes.

P: Correct. And in many instances a person who has committed more than one crime might confess to others, leading police to discover the bodies of victims that are only listed as missing, in exchange for immunity from death sentence prosecution. Think of the families with loved ones unaccounted for. They want closure so that their own psychological healing can begin, but they can't do so unless they know what has actually happened to their friends or family members. If the person has died, they want to know it and to be able to have a funeral and many other things besides. Sometimes a killer knows where bodies are buried or what happened to the victims of crime. The death penalty, by providing a reason for criminals to cooperate, can be used in all these ways. If it helps solve crimes and prevents the death of at least one other innocent person, then I think it has positive benefits.

C: I suppose that's one redeeming thing about capital punishment.

P: Nor is that all. Don't forget that career criminals are often responsible for some of the most horrendous crimes. Those individuals in many cases have already spent the better part of their lives behind bars. They are institutionalized to such a degree that they don't know how to function in free society. That's why they often commit terrible crimes once they're released from prison for one reason or another after serving their sentences. Some of those hardened types are actually more comfortable being in prison after long years of imprisonment, so that the mere threat of being sentenced again to another prison term, even if it means spending the rest of their lives in prison without the possibility of parole, just isn't enough to induce them to cooperate. On the other hand, if they still love life and don't want to be executed, then the death penalty is the last and only means by which judicial authorities can hope to compel them to offer up useful information in exchange for partial immunity.

C: That's not much of a benefit.

P: You were saying that you didn't know of *any* benefits deriving from the death penalty. This is one that law enforcement and judicial officials themselves regard as having important utility. What benefit does society obtain merely from warehousing prisoners for life without the possibility of parole? The law-abiding members of society get nothing whatsoever from that, except perhaps to ease their consciences about not dirtying their hands by endorsing the execution of criminals. I find it ironic that persons who are so concerned about not ending the life of a capital offender seem to have no qualms at all about locking them up and forgetting that they even exist for the rest of their lives. How is that supposed to be more humanitarian? Remember, no matter how good the security at a prison is, there's always the possibility of a dangerous criminal escaping and causing more suffering on the outside until he or she is caught again. That can't happen when the death penalty is implemented.

S: Aren't there other problems that arise through long-term associations between hardened criminals and inmates who have committed lesser crimes or who haven't been breaking the law for as many years?

P: Probably. I don't have any exact information about this, but it makes sense to me to suppose that criminals serving life imprisonment sentences rather than being executed for capital crimes will share their ideas and their general disrespect for society with other prisoners. I imagine that they help to indoctrinate and educate future generations of career criminals who aren't yet serving life terms and will eventually be released. They can be mentored in crime by more hardened criminals, taught ways of evading the law and other aspects of professional crime as part of a growing homicidal subculture. We can limit their influence to at least some extent by implementing the death penalty in the most timely fashion that the law permits, taking the most serious criminals permanently out of circulation.

C: Couldn't those criminals just be kept in solitary confinement?

P: Talk about cruel and unusual punishment. Do you realize that most prisoners suffer lifelong psychological damage and complete mental breakdown even from relatively short stints in solitary confinement? That's no real solution to the problems that are bound to result when the most dangerous criminals associate with other inmates within the prison system. It just breeds more violence.

C: Anyway, I don't think those advantages outweigh the costs. You can talk all you want about fixing the criminal justice system so that you minimize the possibility of executing the wrong person, but I think you know in your heart that there's no possibility of being 100 percent correct, no matter how many safeguards you try to put on the judicial process. And if just one mistake is made, then an innocent person is killed.

S: Yeah, how about that? I thought the whole purpose of the law was to punish persons who commit crimes like willfully causing the death of an innocent person. Who gets punished when the state willfully kills an innocent man or woman on death row?

P: That's an accident that happens within the law, not outside it.

C: Oh, wait a minute. Is that your excuse? You want to say that when an innocent person is killed by some legal process, then there's no recourse? There's no punishment for that sort of wrongful action? Whenever I've heard of anything like this happening, the most that ever occurs is that some official stands in front of a microphone and makes a flat formal apology on television. That's when you can get that much out of them.

Ordinarily, the officials never acknowledge their mistakes. I suppose the governor or somebody sends a letter to the family. So they express their regrets. It doesn't bring the dead person back, doesn't compensate them for the loss. What happens to the scales of Lady Justice then? How is the ideal of perfect justice served when an innocent person is put to death by lethal injection or firing squad or gas or hanging? What brings the balance pans of the justice scales into equilibrium when the state kills an innocent person? You can't suppose that the apology is sufficient, when the family and friends are lucky enough to get one. If that were enough, then it should also be enough for a serial killer to simply apologize for committing murder and causing pain.

If the high ideal of justice to which you aspire requires that capital offenders be put to death, then who do we go after when the state has executed an innocent person? The police? The prosecutors? The judge? The jury members? The prison officials? The executioner? The government officials? The lawmakers? The voters and taxpayers? Who's responsible for that person's death, and who pays the price that you say justice as a noble social ideal requires? I think that you're working under some kind of moral double standard. If I'm understanding you rightly, justice isn't simply justice for all; there's justice for persons who happen to get caught up in the machinery of the judicial system, and then there's an entirely different, let's say, significantly more lenient kind of justice for the judicial system itself and all the people who make it work.

P: I think that there is definitely a difference between a killing that takes place within or outside the law, yes. Look, I would never agree that a murderer who happens to kill a person sentenced to death and awaiting punishment from the state should go scot free because the killer had done the state's job for it by killing the condemned person. That's not justice or what justice requires. I'm talking about ideal justice under the rule of law. There's an important difference between murder and execution.

S: But detectives and the popular media talk about execution-style killings, for example, when mobsters kill people they want eliminated.

P: I can't take account of every popular usage of the word. But calling it "execution *style*" by itself doesn't qualify it as an execution. It just means it's methodical in the way that an execution is supposed to be, it follows the manner associated with that kind of killing.

C: I still think you're operating under a double standard. What counts as justice for an individual doesn't count as justice for society. But society is just made up of individuals, each of whom is also morally responsible for what he or she does.

S: That's certainly true.

C: What happens when a wrongful execution takes place resulting in the death of an innocent person at the hands of the state? Mostly nothing. An apology, maybe. Maybe a study is launched to try to find out what went wrong and how it could be prevented the next time. That's a useful thing, of course, don't get me wrong. But it doesn't seem to serve the ideal of justice that P's been defending. No one gets arrested; no one goes to jail or gets tried and sentenced and convicted and pays for the willful loss of innocent life by forfeiting their own life. That's a double standard.

P: Okay. But there are all sorts of well-justified double standards in almost every moral domain.

C: Like what?

P: Well, you don't hold children to the same moral standard of behavior as you do adults, do you?

C: No.

P: And what about professionals in various fields? We expect different kinds of conduct from doctors and lawyers and architects and engineers than we do from persons who haven't the requisite kinds of training and accreditation, don't we? I mean, for example, if a doctor is on the scene when a person is injured, then we generally expect a qualified professional to act differently than you or I who don't happen to have medical degrees and don't really know what we should or shouldn't do if immediate action is required to save a person's life. If I were to try to help, I might do more harm than good. If a doctor refrains from helping, however, then the doctor is being negligent in his or her responsibilities. That's also a double standard of sorts; but I doubt that you would want to call that principle into question, or want things to be any different.

C: Also true.

P: I wouldn't say that the scales of justice are unevenly tipped when the judicial system accidentally executes the wrong person, regrettable, appalling, and unacceptable as that is, even if no one in the judicial system is put on trial or is in turn sentenced to death for it. There are some very big differences that justify the application of a double standard in this kind of case.

S: What kind of differences?

P: For one thing, the state acts willfully in executing a prisoner in the kinds of situations we've been thinking of but does not willfully, deliberately, or intentionally execute an innocent person. The state executes a person who is believed to be guilty, duly charged, tried, convicted, and sentenced and who later turns out not to have been guilty. That's the deliberate killing of a person who in fact we're supposing to be innocent, but it's an accidental killing of an innocent person since our hypothesis is that the state and its officials do not know that the person is innocent until later when the relevant facts come to light.

S: And what difference does that difference make?

P: It's crucial. Because we also don't sentence ordinary citizens to death for an accidental killing, only for premeditated first-degree murder.

C: I'm not getting this distinction. Suppose that I'm a contract killer working for organized crime and I agree to kill mobster X but accidentally kill mobster Y through a case of mistaken identity; or suppose I accidentally kill someone Z who's not connected with the criminal element at all, just an average person minding his or her own business who ends up being in the wrong place at the wrong time. You're not going to say that as a contract killer in that case I'm not morally responsible or that I wouldn't be held responsible before the law for killing Y or Z when I had intended to kill X, are you? Surely, I'll be just as morally and legally responsible for taking a life in either of those two cases as if I succeeded in hitting the target of my murder contract.

P: I guess that's right.

C: So, forget about that difference between the killer and the state when it accidentally executes an innocent person for a capital crime that the person didn't really commit. And, of course, I mean by the state the individuals who are working for the state in the judicial system and under its authority.

S: I think you've got P on the run, C. What's the justification for the double standard now?

P: Let's look at the motives of those involved in the killings in both kinds of cases. The contract killer wants to earn a fee.

S: The state employee working in the judicial system also wants to earn a salary.

C: Right.

P: But the contract killer has no social authorization for killing another person, and employees in the judicial system do.

C: What difference does that make? You say yourself that society is just an organized collection of individuals. Well, organized crime, as the name itself implies, is an organized collection of individuals. Anyway, the contract killer is authorized, if you want to put it that way, by the society or subculture of the members of organized crime who hire the killer to assassinate the victim.

P: Actually, I don't want to say that the contract killer is authorized to assassinate. And by "society" I don't just mean any organized collection of persons working in concert with some sort of hierarchy or chain of command. I mean society as a whole, the established social entity that determines the rule of law.

S: The establishment, then, is it?

C: See, I don't think that's going to float. If by "society" you just mean the dominant social group, then we come back to your own examples about the moral justification of aberrant societies like the Nazis. They were established and fully in power, and they authorized all kinds of killings that most reflective people reject as morally indefensible.

S: Right. It can't just be the numbers of persons in official capacities within a social structure that determines moral legitimacy in your sense. What would you say in that case about a resistance movement to the Nazis? They're fewer in number, they don't really have any official or officially recognized power. Let's suppose that they're the good guys, and they're doing their best to fight the oppression and overthrow a morally corrupt regime, even if that means assassinating certain members of the ruling party . . .

P: Wait . . . you're not trying to compare the mafia to an opposition group trying to depose the Third Reich, are you? That's not an analogy anyone is going to be able to take seriously.

S: No, of course not. I'm just trying to point out that so far you haven't said enough to distinguish between legitimate and illegitimate social authority. It's not merely the numbers or being in power or having the governmental seal in your control. There's something more to it than that if we're talking about moral legitimacy and moral authority.

P: You're right. Well, how about if I simply said that what distinguishes the established authority of society administering the death penalty under the law in the United States and a criminal organization is that the government is elected by a majority of citizens in a free election and is subject to a variety of checks and balances on the exercise of its power, that it exists for the sake of promoting independently justifiable moral and social values, none of which is true by hypothesis of organized crime.

C: That's better, I think. But I hope you're not saying that with that sort of legitimization the judicial system of an established social order is free to do whatever it wants with no oversight or accountability.

P: Certainly not. I want to hold the judicial system fully responsible for whatever mistakes it makes in wrongly executing capital criminals. Here's another point. It's not as though I don't think there are any circumstances under which a government representative of the judiciary could be held morally and legally responsible for the wrongful execution of a prisoner. In particular, I think that persons working for the judicial system could even be arrested, tried, convicted, and sentenced to death for the wrongful execution of an innocent person on death row and be executed themselves for what they've done.

S: How would that work?

P: It would have to happen because the person was deliberately and knowingly involved in a wrongful execution. For example, suppose that I'm a prosecutor and I know that an accused person is innocent but bring the person to trial anyway because I can gain something for myself by doing it. Maybe I want to steal the person's spouse, or I want to inherit money that I can't receive unless the person is out of the way, or I want to advance my career as a prosecutor and don't care how I do it. Or suppose I'm a judge or jury member with the same kinds of motive. Or the executioner or another kind of prison official, and information comes to light about the condemned person's innocence that I deliberately withhold in order to profit in some way by the person's death. Then I would say that in those representative kinds of cases—and probably many others besides—merely working for the government would not make the individual responsible for the execution of an innocent person immune from prosecution and punishment, including capital punishment in the form of the death penalty.

The killer in that case is using the machinery of the justice system to his or her own ends as an instrument to deliberately and with cold-blooded premeditation murder an innocent person. Such a wrongdoer should be as much subject to the full penalties of the law as if he or she had used a gun or a knife or poison or a speeding automobile or any other murder weapon to kill. Working for the judicial system in any capacity is no excuse and no protection for a murderer responsible for the death of an innocent person on death row executed by the state if the execution occurs under these kinds of circumstances. There's no impunity in my book for someone who abuses the death penalty and attempts to use their official status in the judicial system as a cover for first-degree murder. Still, I have to say that I'm considering this only as a very remote possibility. It could be the dramatic premise for a fascinating detective movie, but I don't think it happens very often if at all in real life. There are lots of checks and balances in the system, internal and external, and there are watchdogs looking out especially for any hint of a conflict of interest on the part of persons involved in the implementation of capital punishment.

C: Is that so? I'd like to believe that was true . . .

P: Anyway, my point is that I don't offer a blank check to persons involved in the management of convicted capital offenders when an innocent person is executed. If it's truly an accident, then I think that there should be a thorough investigation and appropriate safeguards implemented and enforced. If there was some collusion that can be demonstrated in a court of law against persons involved in the process, then I think they should be prosecuted to the law's fullest extent. If they are found guilty and properly sentenced to death, then I believe that they should be subject to execution themselves.

S: Do you think that's enough to escape the objection that you're accepting a double standard?

P: Remember, I don't deny that there's a double standard. I just think that in this case as in many other situations, a double standard is morally justified. One must often distinguish between different kinds of appropriate circumstances in order to make correct, nuanced judgments. Justice isn't always a matter of one size fits all. Acting on behalf of the morally and legally legitimate authority of the government, assuming that there's no subversion of the criminal justice system for personal ends, puts a prison or other judicial official in a very different category from an ordinary person outside the system acting violently for wrongful purposes, even if his or her actions in both cases happen to result in the deliberate killing of an innocent person or a person who turns out later to have been innocent.

C: To me this all seems very troublesome. It sounds as though you're making exceptions for someone going to their death at the hands of the state and allowing the scales of justice to be tipped out of balance. What makes up for the death of an innocent death row prisoner when he or she is wrongly executed?

P: Nothing ever makes up for the loss of a human life. I've admitted that from the start. There's no problem about balancing the justice scales in the case of an accidental execution of an innocent person precisely because it's an accident. Assuming that the execution occurs not as a result of negligence but as an honest mistake within the whole judicial process that isn't discovered or rectified in time, then there's no act of wrongdoing on the part of the justice system and hence no crime and no punishment to be assigned. If the execution occurs because someone deliberately abuses the justice system in order to commit murder by legal execution of someone on death row, as unlikely as that might be, then whoever is responsible for the execution has committed a crime and ought to be arrested, tried, sentenced, and convicted and, if the facts and application of the law warrants it, possibly even executed for first-degree murder. It is only in the second case that the question of balancing the justice scales pans arises, and there I think that justice should impartially prosecute whoever is responsible for the execution of the innocent person just as if another kind of weapon was used to end that person's life.

S: It all sounds a little too clean and simple.

P: Only in theory. In practice, of course, it's as difficult as any other legal proceeding. There are always many opportunities for things to go wrong. What I would want to insist on is that as long as no one is using the judicial system for his or her own criminal purposes, then there's no problem about trying to approximate the ideal of justice in the implementation of capital punishment when an innocent person is wrongly, accidentally, executed. Nor am I trying to downplay the horror of someone's being executed by mistake. It's a terrible consequence of the attempt to fulfill the requirements of justice as they pertain to the execution of individuals who have committed certain types of capital crimes. It's to be avoided at all costs. I don't want anyone to be wrongfully executed. But I also don't want persons who are guilty of serious crimes to go unpunished or to receive an insufficient punishment that does not adequately reflect the enormity of their crimes.

S: I suppose this is a moot question, but I imagine you would also want to see the death penalty applied to people who commit acts of domestic terrorism, as well as foreign terrorists, if we can get our hands on them. Is that right?

P: Honestly, I don't have any opinion about who specifically should or should not be subject to capital punishment. That's for the courts to decide. I think, for example, that the decision to execute Timothy McVeigh, who was found guilty of the 1995 Oklahoma City bombing, was probably morally justified. He killed 168 people, including children playing in a day care center at the Alfred P. Murrah Federal Building, and all for some tragically misguided and misinformed beliefs he had about the government's incursions on rights and individual liberties of American citizens following the 1993 Waco siege in Texas. Undoubtedly, the government, the Federal Bureau of Alcohol, Tobacco, and Firearms, didn't handle that situation at the Branch Davidian religious cult compound as well as it should have. But I think most people will agree that McVeigh didn't have the right as a result to kill innocent people in retaliation. It was murder and terrorism, the worst case of terrorism ever perpetrated on American soil until the al-Qaeda attacks on the World Trade Center Twin Towers in Manhattan on September 11, 2001. I think I agree with the death sentence in McVeigh's case, and I take that as a relatively clear-cut case of the kind of crime for which capital punishment is not only appropriate but absolutely required by the interests of justice.

S: So, let me ask you something, C. Do you think that McVeigh should have been imprisoned for life without the possibility of parole instead of being executed?

C: You know by now I do.

S: Because I think I feel like P that for crimes of that sort there's no other proper punishment than execution. How was he executed, exactly?

P: Lethal injection. He was allowed to have a prerequiem musical service performed. He had a Catholic chaplain in attendance. And he had a last meal consisting of two pints of mint chocolate chip ice cream. That's a lot more than his victims had, all of whom were taken completely by surprise by the sudden explosion that brought down the Murrah Building.

C: But why do you think it was right to execute him?

S: His actions made him a symbol for other terrorists. By staying alive in prison, he would be the subject of occasional media attention. He could try to communicate with persons within and outside of prison and possibly have some effect or even control over their actions that might have led to similar acts of terrorism.

P: All that's true, I think. But even if he could have been so tightly monitored and controlled during the rest of his life in prison so that he could never have gotten a message out to the rest of the world and even if he could have been surrounded with a total news blackout so that no one ever heard another word from or about him while he was alive, the main thing is that I think he deserved to die for what he did. It's as simple as that. His actions caused so much misery and destruction to the lives of others that he deserved to die as a result and that was the only adequate punishment he could have possibly received.

C: Aren't you two making yourselves into judge and jury?

P: Well, McVeigh had a judge and jury, and this is what they decided should be his fate under the applicable laws. Myself, I'm just offering my opinion on the outcome, as S asked me to do.

S: Same here.

C: And if you had been the judge or been asked to serve on the jury?

S: It's all hypothetical. It would depend on what I would have actually heard offered as evidence and arguments in the court. I think on the basis of what I know through the news media when I was following the case with some attention at the time that I wouldn't have had any real moral reservations about voting for his conviction knowing that it would probably result in his execution. I don't think I would have hesitated to vote guilty. Nor do I think I would have had any moral problems officiating in his execution, although it's really not the kind of thing I can imagine myself personally doing. Still, I'm glad that there are persons who can do what sometimes needs to be done to put away criminals, especially terrorists, who commit the kinds of crimes of which McVeigh was convicted.

P: Likewise.

S: This is also where I differ with P. I think I would prefer to see the death penalty reserved only for the most extreme acts of violence and only where the evidence is absolutely incontrovertible. I'm sensitive to what C says about not always knowing with full certainty that a person convicted of a capital crime is actually guilty, although I believe that the death penalty ought to be maintained as a possible punishment for the worst offenders. I think there are definitely too many persons on death row. I'm greatly concerned about the fact that many persons sentenced to death and who could have been executed have later been released because it turned out that they were innocent all along, and I'm concerned about the extent to which capital punishment is decided on the basis of emotional and other circumstantial factors that can affect the decisions of a judge or jury but that don't always reflect the real merits of a case. I'd like to see some reform of the current practices.

C: Like what?

S: I think that many states in the United States allow too broad a spectrum of categories of crime that can be punished by death. I think that there should be some limiting of the types of crime that can carry the death sentence and that this should be applied nationwide.

P: I'm not sure I understand what you mean. Are you saying, for example, that killing three people should not make you eligible for a death sentence but that killing four might? Are you suggesting that we assign numbers to determine when the death penalty can and cannot apply? Or is it the way in which the victims are killed that should matter? If it's a quick and painless death, should that be a factor? Do the motives for the crime make a difference?

S: I don't know. I'm only reacting to the fact that it strikes me that there are far too many people awaiting execution and that capital punishment for a crime should be considered only for the absolutely worst kinds of criminal offenses.

P: I doubt that many prosecutors would agree with you. It might be unconstitutional in the first place to try to legislate limits for the death penalty that would apply to all states. There are issues of states' rights that enter into this kind of deliberation. Also, I think that many law enforcement agents and prosecutors would not want there to be hard-and-fast rules about who can and cannot be sentenced to death because it gives criminals too much of an advantage knowing what they'll be able to get away with if they're caught.

S: So, you're saying that the police and judicial system want maximum flexibility in sentencing?

P: I think so, yes. Some of them. Besides, if there are too many people on death row, it's no doubt because there are too many people committing serious crimes. I don't think anyone is on death row for grand theft auto or shoplifting. We need to address the deeper reasons in society that have fostered a criminal subculture, and we need to try to prevent crime before it happens. That's where I think we ought to be devoting our attention and our resources. Then we wouldn't have to worry about how many condemned criminals are awaiting execution. Capital punishment should serve as a last resort for only the most outrageous crimes, and, hopefully, there wouldn't be anyone actually awaiting execution at all. I don't want anyone to die as the result of homicide or capital punishment. But if there are persons who are willing to commit acts of murder and terrorism, then I think that we can aspire to the ideals of a just society only by maintaining and occasionally implementing a death penalty. I don't see any other way in which we can preserve the kind of society that protects as many individual liberties as ours and still acts to defend the lives of innocent persons from wrongdoers who want to abuse their liberties by infringing on the moral and legal right to life of others.

C: You and S can agree about this all you want. There's no way I will ever resign myself to the morality of capital punishment. I don't think Timothy McVeigh should have been executed. When you execute these people, they just become legends and martyrs for the extremists who follow them. On top of that, society loses the positive publicity it can get when these types, as they almost all eventually do, mellow out in prison and finally express remorse for what they've done. Anyway, I still think that society stoops to their level when it executes murderers and terrorists.

P: Are you equating the rule of law with murder and terror?

C: Not at all. What I'm saying is that when both criminals and the law resort to violence in order to achieve their aims, then in the minds of many people it validates the kinds of methods that murderers and terrorists use. I think that society should be setting a higher standard and better example by refusing to take a person's life regardless of what the person may have done. The only way that we can ever make moral progress is through education, and the best way to educate persons not to commit acts of violence is to provide a positive role model in which problems are solved in nonviolent ways.

S: Do you think of execution by lethal injection as violent?

C: Whether it's violent or not, I'm talking about not succumbing to the emotional desire for revenge against persons who have acted antisocially in taking human life. The very thing that P thinks of as the ideal of justice where capital offenders are concerned strikes me as just the opposite. It's a reaction of anger and frustration. The ideal of justice is to lead society gently in the path we want it to follow. To me that means not allowing any state-sanctioned killing except in cases of self-defense.

P: I could almost accept that position, except that I think we disagree about when society is and when it isn't under attack and when and how we need to defend ourselves from internal and external enemies.

C: As bad as McVeigh was, he didn't and he couldn't do anything to threaten the safety of society as such. When we implement the death penalty against murderers and terrorists, we send them and all their potential followers a message—a signal that says we consider them so dangerous that we think we need to take the most extreme possible measures to contain them. Don't you see? That just gives them more psychological power and encourages them to try more and more violent methods. After all, some murderers and terrorists are either so desperate or so committed to their causes that they don't really care whether they are caught and imprisoned or executed. They are going to try to do what they believe they need to do no matter how hard we try to stop them. What we can do is not to allow their actions to degrade our behavior and determine the course of our way of life by engaging in killing as a response.

S: Are you talking about turning the other cheek?

C: Absolutely not. I'm talking about catching criminals and terrorists and locking them up for good where they can't hurt anyone ever again. I do not condone letting them off easy for their crimes, but I also don't want the society that I live in and that I love to lower itself to anything even remotely approaching their level by taking human life as a way of pursuing a social policy agenda. We don't need to kill people in order to protect ourselves from people who kill people. When we try to do so, we weave a deep contradiction of values and principles into the very fabric of our society that must ultimately have disastrous effects. I think that we are hurting ourselves in a very real but subtle way when we impose the death penalty against those who fail to respect other persons' moral right to life.

P: I haven't even made a dent in your position that the moral right to life is unconditional, have I?

C: No.

S: P, I'm shocked. Do you think that the right to life is *conditional*?

P: I do. I think that you can give up your right to life by demonstrating supreme contempt for the moral right to life of others. C and I have been all over this already. What do you think about it?

S: I don't know what to think. I used to believe I had fairly clear ideas about whether the death penalty was morally justified. That's why I agreed to work on this project as research assistant. Now, I guess I'm no longer so sure. How on earth do we decide these things, whether the moral right to life is conditional or unconditional? That seems to me to be the crux of the matter. If the right to life is unconditional, then those who profess to respect the moral right to life cannot consistently infringe against that right by supporting a death penalty. On the other hand, who's to say that the right to life isn't conditional, that an individual can lose the right to life by failing to respect the moral right to life of other persons?

C: That's exactly the impasse we've encountered.

P: Is that the answer, then? Some people believe that the right to life can never be justifiably violated, and others think that the right to life depends on how we live and in particular on how we act toward others? It would represent progress in our discussion if we could come away from all this exchange with the sense that this at least is how the dispute takes shape. When you cut through all the arguments about costs and deterrence, reform and recidivism, irreversibility of mistaken judgment, and all the rest, does it all just boil down to a difference of opinion about whether or not the right to life is something that can be relinquished?

S: I don't know. Maybe. I'm not sure.

P: I'm beginning to think that our frontal approach to the problem is really not getting us anywhere. If we have such a fundamental, irresolvable conflict of intuitions about the nature of the moral right to life, a collision between insights as to whether the moral right to life is conditional or unconditional, if we have hit some kind of stalemate here, then perhaps we ought to try another kind of tactic altogether.

C: Such as?

S: Hey, there's the sign for the art museum.

P: This is our exit.

Selected Readings
for Further Study

Acker, James R, and David R. Karp, eds. *Wounds That Do Not Bind: Victim-Based Perspectives on the Death Penalty*. Durham, NC: Carolina Academic Press, 2006.

Acker, James R., Robert M. Bohm, and Charles S. Lanier, eds. *America's Experiment with Capital Punishment: Reflections on the Past, Present, and Future of the Ultimate Penal Sanction*. 2nd ed. Durham, NC: Carolina Academic Press, 2003.

Anckar, Carsten. *Determinants of the Death Penalty: A Comparative Study of the World*. New York: Routledge, 2004.

Atwell, Mary Welek. *Wretched Sisters: Examining Gender and Capital Punishment*. New York: Peter Lang, 2007.

Bae, Sangmin. *When the State No Longer Kills: International Human Rights Norms and Abolition of Capital Punishment*. Albany: State University of New York Press, 2007.

Baird, Robert M., and Stuart E. Rosenbaum, eds. *Punishment and the Death Penalty: The Current Debate*. Amherst, NY: Prometheus Books, 1995.

Banner, Stuart. *The Death Penalty: An American History*. Cambridge, MA: Harvard University Press, 2003.

Beck, Elizabeth, Sarah Britto, and Arlene Andrews. *In the Shadow of Death: Restorative Justice and Death Row Families*. New York: Oxford University Press, 2007.

Bedau, Hugo Adam, ed. *The Death Penalty in America: Current Controversies*. New York: Oxford University Press, 1998.

Bedau, Hugo Adam. *Killing as Punishment: Reflections on the Death Penalty in America*. Boston: Northeastern University Press, 2004.

Bedau, Hugo Adam, and Paul Cassell, eds. *Debating the Death Penalty: Should America Have Capital Punishment? The Experts on Both Sides Make Their Best Case*. New York: Oxford University Press, 2003.

Berns, Walter. *For Capital Punishment: Crime and the Morality of the Death Penalty*. Lanham, MD: University Press of America, 1991.

Bessler, John D. *Kiss of Death: America's Love Affair with the Death Penalty.* Boston: Northeastern University Press, 2003.

Brugger, E. Christian. *Capital Punishment and Roman Catholic Moral Education.* Notre Dame, IN: University of Notre Dame Press, 2003.

Burger, Dan. *Death Row: Profiles of 12 Condemned Killers, Capital Punishment Legislation, Complete Listing of 2,457 Death Row Inmates, Vol. 2, No. 1.* Carlsbad, CA: Glenn Hare Publishers, 1991.

Cohen, Stanley. *The Wrong Men: America's Epidemic of Wrongful Death Row Convictions.* New York: Carroll & Graf Publishers, 2003.

Connors, Paul G. *Capital Punishment.* San Diego: Greenhaven Press, 2007.

Costanzo, Mark. *Just Revenge: Costs and Consequences of the Death Penalty.* W. H. Freeman, 1997.

Coyne, Randall, and Lyn Entzeroth. *Capital Punishment and the Judicial Process (Carolina Academic Press Law Casebook).* Durham, NC: Carolina Academic Press, 2001.

Culbert, Jennifer L. *Dead Certainty: The Death Penalty and the Problem of Judgment.* Palo Alto, CA: Stanford University Press, 2008.

Donohue, John J. *Uses and Abuses of Empirical Evidence in the Death Penalty Debate.* Chicago: National Bureau of Economic Research, 2006.

Dow, David, and Mark Dow. *Machinery of Death: The Reality of America's Death Penalty Regime.* New York: Routledge, 2002.

Dulles, Avery Cardinal. "Catholicism and Capital Punishment." *First Things: The Journal of Religion, Culture, and Public Life,* 112 (2001): 30–35.

Edelman, Bryan C. *Racial Prejudice, Juror Empathy, and Sentencing in Death Penalty Cases.* New York: LFB Scholarly Publications, 2006.

Elster, Jean Alicia. *The Death Penalty.* San Diego: Greenhaven Press, 2005.

Fisanick, Nick. *The Ethics of Capital Punishment.* San Diego: Greenhaven Press, 2005.

Fleury-Steiner, Benjamin. *Jurors' Stories of Death: How America's Death Penalty Invests in Inequality.* Ann Arbor: University of Michigan Press, 2004.

Friedman, Lauri S. *The Death Penalty.* San Diego, CA: Daniel A. Leone, 2007.

Fuhrman, Mark. *Death and Justice: An Exposé of Oklahoma's Death Row Machine.* New York: William Morrow, 2003.

Garvey, Stephen P. *Beyond Repair? America's Death Penalty* (Constitutional Conflicts). Durham, NC: Duke University Press, 2002.

Gerber, Rudolph J. *The Top Ten Death Penalty Myths: The Politics of Crime Control.* Westport, CT: Praeger Publishers, 2007.

Gershman, Gary P. *Death Penalty on Trial: A Handbook with Cases, Laws, and Documents.* Santa Barbara, CA: ABC-CLIO, 2005.

Hanks, Gardner C. *Against the Death Penalty: Christian and Secular Arguments against Capital Punishment.* Scottdale, PA: Herald Press, 1997.

Heilbrun, Alfred B. *The Death Penalty: Beyond the Smoke and Mirrors.* Lanham, MD: University Press of America, 2006.

Henningfeld, Diane Andrews. *The Death Penalty: Opposing Viewpoints.* San Diego: Greenhaven Press, 2006.

Hood, Roger G. *The Death Penalty: Beyond Abolition.* Council of Europe Publications, 2004.

Hood, Roger. *The Death Penalty: A Worldwide Perspective.* 3rd ed. New York: Oxford University Press, 2002.

Kay, Judith W. *Murdering Myths: The Story Behind the Death Penalty.* Lanham, MD: Rowman & Littlefield, 2005.

Keyzer, Amy Marcaccio. *Does Capital Punishment Deter Crime?* San Diego: Greenhaven Press, 2007.

King, Rachel. *The Death Penalty for Teens: A Pro/Con Issue.* Berkeley Heights, NJ: Endlow Publishing, 2000.

King, Rachel. *Don't Kill in Our Names: Families of Murder Victims Speak Out Against the Death Penalty.* New Brunswick, NJ: Rutgers University Press, 2003.

Kudlac, Christopher S. *Public Executions: The Death Penalty and the Media.* Westport, CT: Praeger Publishers, 2007.

Kukathas, Uma. *Death Penalty.* San Diego: Greenhaven Press, 2008.

Kurtis, Bill. *The Death Penalty on Trial: Crisis in American Justice.* New York: Public Affairs, 2004.

Latzner, Barry, ed. *Death Penalty Cases.* 2nd ed. Oxford: Butterworth-Heinemann, 2002.

Lifton, Robert Jay, and Greg Mitchell. *Who Owns Death? Capital Punishment, the American Conscience, and the End of Executions.* New York: HarperPerennial, 2002.

Lu, Hong. *China's Death Penalty: History, Law, and Contemporary Practices.* London: Routledge, 2007.

Mandery, Evan J. *Capital Punishment: A Balanced Examination.* Boston: Jones & Bartlett Publishers, 2005.

Martinez, J. Michael, William D. Richardson, and D. Brandon Hornsby. *The Leviathan's Choice: Capital Punishment in the Twenty-First Century.* Lanham, MD: Rowman & Littlefield, 2002.

Massingill, Ruth. *Prison City: Life with the Death Penalty in Huntsville, Texas.* Bern: Peter Lang, 2007.

Mello, Michael A. *Dead Wrong: A Death Row Lawyer Speaks Out against Capital Punishment.* Madison: University of Wisconsin Press, 1999.

Miller, Karen S. *Wrongful Capital Convictions and the Legitimacy of the Death Penalty.* New York: LFB Scholarly Publications, 2006.

Ogletree, Charles J. *From Lynch Mobs to the Killing State: Race and the Death Penalty in America.* New York: New York University Press, 2006.

Owens, Erik C. *Religion and the Death Penalty: A Call for Reckoning.* Grand Rapids, MI: W. B. Eerdmans, 2004.

Prejean, Helen. *Dead Man Walking: An Eyewitness Account of the Death Penalty in the United States.* New York: Vintage Books, 1996.

Rothchild, Jonathan. *Doing Justice to Mercy: Religion, Law, and Criminal Justice.* Charlottesville: University Press of Virginia, 2007.

Sarat, Austin. *The Cultural Lives of Capital Punishment: Comparative Perspectives.* Palo Alto, CA: Stanford University Press, 2005.

Sarat, Austin. *The Death Penalty: Influences and Outcomes.* Aldershot: Ashgate, 2005.

Sarat, Austin. *When the State Kills: Capital Punishment and the American Condition.* Princeton, NJ: Princeton University Press, 2002.

Sharp, Susan F. *Hidden Victims: The Effects of the Death Penalty on Families of the Accused.* New Brunswick, NJ: Rutgers University Press, 2005.

Smith, D. P., and Michael L. Varnado. *Loss of Faith: The Dead Man Walking's Forgotten Victims.* Lincoln, NE: Writers Advantage, 2002.

Sorensen, Jonathan R. *Lethal Injection: Capital Punishment in Texas During the Modern Era*. Austin: University of Texas Press, 2006.

Stack, Richard A. *Dead Wrong: Violence, Vengeance, and the Victims of Capital Punishment*. Westport, CT: Praeger Publishers, 2006.

Steelwater, Eliza. *The Hangman's Knot: Lynching, Legal Execution, and America's Struggle with the Death Penalty*. Boulder, CO: Westview Press, 2003.

Streib, Victor L. *Death Penalty in a Nutshell*. Eagan, MN: Thomson/West, 2005.

Streib, Victor L. *The Fairer Death: Executing Women in Ohio*. Athens: Ohio University Press, 2006.

Sundby, Scott E. *A Life and Death Decision: A Jury Weighs the Death Penalty*. New York: Palgrave Macmillan, 2005.

Turow, Scott. *Ultimate Punishment: A Lawyer's Reflections on Dealing with the Death Penalty*. New York: Farrar, Straus & Giroux, 2003.

United States Congress, Committee on the Judiciary. Subcommittee on Crime, Terrorism, and Homeland Security. *Death Penalty Reform Act of 2006: Hearing Before the Subcommittee on Crime, Terrorism, and Homeland Security of the Committee on the Judiciary, House of Representatives, One Hundred Ninth Congress, Second Session, on H.R. 5040, March 30, 2006*. United States. Congress. House. Washington, DC: U.S. Government Printing Office, 2006.

United States Congress. Senate Committee on the Judiciary. Subcommittee on the Constitution, Civil Rights, and Property Rights. *An Examination of the Death Penalty in the United States: Hearing before the Subcommittee on the Constitution, Civil Rights, and Property Rights of the Committee on the Judiciary, United States Senate, One Hundred Ninth Congress, Second Session*, February 1, 2006. United States. Congress. Senate. U.S. Government Printing Office, 2006.

Vila, Bryan, and Cynthia Morris, eds. *Capital Punishment in the United States: A Documentary History*. Westport, CT: Greenwood Press, 1997.

Von Hirsch, Andrew. *Censure and Sanctions*. Oxford: Clarendon Press, 1993.

Von Hirsch, Andrew. *Past or Future Crimes: Deservedness and Dangerousness in Sentencing*. New Brunswick, NJ: Rutgers University Press, 1985.

Von Hirsch, Andrew. *Proportionate Sentencing: Exploring the Principles*. New York: Oxford University Press, 2005.

Williams, Mary E. *Capital Punishment*. San Diego: Greenhaven Press, 2005.

Williams, Mary E. *Is the Death Penalty Fair?* San Diego: Greenhaven Press, 2003.

Zimring, Franklin E. *The Contradictions of American Capital Punishment*. New York: Oxford University Press, 2003.

About the Author

Dale Jacquette is Lehrstuhl ordentlicher Professor für Philosophie, Schwerpunkt theoretische Philosophie (Senior Professorial Chair in Theoretical Philosophy), at Universität Bern, Switzerland. He is the author of numerous articles on logic, metaphysics, philosophy of mind, and aesthetics and has recently published *Ontology*, *David Hume's Critique of Infinity*, *The Philosophy of Schopenhauer*, and *Journalistic Ethics: Moral Responsibility in the Media*.